Lakeside

Book Three

THE
UNFORTUNATE CARP!

and Other Watery Tales

CARL EWALD

Translations and Adaptations
William V. Zucker

Illustrations
Subhadeep Ghosh

© 2021WILLIAM V. ZUCKER / Translator

Available in these formats:
978-1-7357216-4-4 (Paperback)
978- 1-7357216-5-1 (eBook)

Library of Congress Control Number: 2020919159

Editing: Graham W. Schofield

Cover Design/Illustrations: Subhadeep Ghosh

Published by the translator...
Forgeus Press / Tucson, Arizona 85716U.S.A.
Phone: 520-327-0192

williamzucker@msn.com

classicnaturestoriesforkids.com

Other Translations by William V. Zucker

To Michele

...for all the love and constancy.

Translator's Introduction...

In this third book of short nature stories, Carl Ewald (1856-1908) opens up the mysteries of what really goes on around—and under—a 'peaceful' lake. Whether it is cute tadpoles, swimming innocently near the lake's shore, or a larva waiting impatiently to become an adult dragonfly, each participant offers its own learning for children. But there is a key lesson that one hopes will take root: that the often seemingly cruel, amoral, unthinking indifference of nature is what it is. Nature has no favorites!

Even in the environment of a serene lake, there are competing forces at work in the interplay between plants and animals. Whether it's in the eel's manner of reproduction, showing unfeeling nonchalance for its progeny, or on the contrary, the deep regard the mayfly has for its offspring, there is much contrast to see. Then there's the clam and the crayfish that share a common problem.

In the fourth book to follow (*The Invincible Sea*), readers will discover what happens in the oceans of the world, where dynamic forces are continuously at work, and where the life cycles of the different sea life are the determining factors in survival of the fittest. Or where, sometimes, the dominating factor is the sheer randomness inherent in the environment.

My sincerest thanks to Lis Pilgaard for help with translation chores. For invaluable guidance and help with the text, I thank

Graham Schofield, and to Subhadeep Ghosh, my sincerest gratitude for his outstanding illustrations and book cover design, but especially for his patience and appreciation of how text and visuals need to coalesce.

William V. Zucker
Tucson, Arizona - U.S.A.
2021

When you finish reading this book... would you please write a review!

Authors (and translators)
love hearing from their readers.

To help other readers and children find these realistic descriptions of nature by Carl Ewald, please let the translator know what you thought about the stories in this book.

Please leave an honest review on Amazon or Goodreads or your other preferred online store.

(If you are under 14, please ask a grown-up to help you).

Thank you!

P.S. Please mention what your favorite story was.
www.amazon.com
www.classicnaturestoriesforkids.com

Choose your story...

THE UNFORTUNATE CARP!

The Beginning

One early spring morning, a young reed-warbler was sitting in a bush in Italy feeling sorry for himself. He had nothing to complain about since the sun was shining, there were plenty of flies, and there were no predators around to harm him. Indeed, a moment ago, a pretty girl with dark eyes sat under a bush listening to his song and sending a loving kiss to him. Still, something was lacking, and he grew tired of the Italian flies.

He had a feeling he could fly hundreds of miles without a break, and there were sounds in his throat that he could not get out. His heart was full of sad longings he didn't comprehend, and which would have made him cry, but reed-warblers don't cry. The only thing he could do was to sing. And for that, one day is as good as another, whether you are happy or sad.

So, he sang awhile, and when he stopped, he heard a tweet from a nearby bush which sounded just like his own, only a little quieter. He quickly hopped down to a lower branch and gazed at the sweetest, cutest little reed-warbler female that he could imagine. No one was there to make introductions, which they did themselves, since there isn't so much formality among birds; introductions are also over more quickly, and after they had conversed for five minutes, he said:

"After seeing you, I know what is wrong with me. I am homesick for the country of my birth. I remember so clearly the peaceful lake with reeds and rushes and the green beech trees."

"I'm also homesick," she replied. "I remember it too."

"Then let's fly there together," he said. "As soon as we reach the lake, we'll settle down in some friendly place and build our nest. How does that sound?"

"Will you cherish me until death?" she asked.

"I can't promise beyond this summer," he replied. "But I do promise you that."

"Okay," she said: "I will be your mate," but there was no one to announce their decision to because they had seen none of their families since the fall. They held a little private party, feasting on some fat ants that he caught, sang a little duet, and then started on their way.

They flew for many days and rested up when they found a green valley, for there were many of them traveling the same routes, and they often flew as a large flock. But the reed-warbler twosome always kept close together as becoming a loving couple. When they grew tired, they cheered each other up by telling stories about the little lake.

*   *   *

They finally arrived one lovely day at the end of May. The sun was shining, and white clouds drifted softly in the sky. The beeches had already budded out, and the oaks were about to. The reeds and rushes were green, and the slight waves leaped for joy in the lake as everything radiated happiness.

"Isn't it lovely here," said the male reed-warbler.

"Yes, it is," she said. "Let us build our nest here."

Close to the banks, they found a place they both liked. They tied three reeds together with fine threads a foot above the water and they wove the cutest little basket nest which they lined with the softest down. When the reeds swayed in the wind, the nest swayed too, but nothing happened because they tied the nest well together, and reed-warblers never get sea-sick.

It took them a week to make it, and during that time they were deliriously happy together, and one could hear their singing around the whole lake. In the evening when they became tired, they flitted around in the reeds, flirting with each other, or peeking in at the neighbors.

"The water lily is shooting up through the water," said the reed-warbler. "I remember it well; it's so elegant and lovely."

"And there's a green frog sitting on the bank," remarked her mate. "It's snapping up flies and larvae just like I am, but there's enough for all of us so we can still be friends."

As she continued to explore the water below, suddenly she screamed: "There are crayfish crawling down there, and there goes the roach fish and the perch... there's a whole green forest at the bottom of the lake! The fish are swimming among the submerged branches, and fly larvae are bobbing in their larval cases."

"Yes, it's lovely here," he said as if he owned it all. And she added: "Everyone is so happy. I'm sure there must be many loving couples like us."

"Of course," answered her mate. "In the spring, many species choose partners and pair up. But I really don't think anyone in the entire world is as happy as we are."

He thrust his neck forward and sang until it resounded:

> *There's no one in the world*
> *With a lover like mine,*
> *So sweet and so fine,*
> *With a voice to behold.*
>
> *Let the others swoon,*
> *For whoever they will,*
> *My lover is mine 'til*
> *Her very last trill.*

"Will you only love me for this summer?" she asked.
"That's what I'm told," he said.

A Big Braggart

Reed-warbler sighed deeply five times, and with each sigh, she laid an egg. Afterwards, she squatted on top of the eggs and sighed some more. The reeds swayed in the gentle breeze along with the nest and the cute little brown mother bird sitting on the eggs. Even her mate swayed, because he was sitting on a nearby rush weed, and when one of them swayed, all the others did too.

"It's no worse for you than for the others, dearest," he said. "Peek down into the water and see how busy the others are too."

"I can't see anything now," she replied, "nor will I be able to observe a thing for four weeks," she said sadly.

"Tut, tut," said the reed-warbler. "You can peek a little as soon as you give the eggs a shuffle and snuggle down again quickly."

So, she peeked, and sure enough, it was busy enough down there. The marsh snail with her course shell was swimming around on the surface of the water. Then, she tipped herself up, and with her head in the water, her shell became a boat-like float with her broad foot above, keeping the body vertical. Then she straightened up even more, so the boat-like appendage disappeared, and she sank to the bottom where she stuck a total mess of slimy eggs onto a stalk of a waterlily.

A pike came by and laid an egg in the waving, submerged plants. The carp did the same, and the perch hung an attractive clump of eggs between the reeds where the reed-warblers had built their nest. The frog appeared with her eggs, the sticklebacks had their nest almost ready, and hundreds of animals so small you could hardly see them, were running around, getting prepared for birthing time.

"Those poor mothers," said mother-to-be reed-warbler. "They have a tough time of it and...",

Suddenly, an eel lifted its head out of the muck and interrupted: "I've moved around in this world... believe me," and disappeared.

"I don't like that intruder," she yelled to her mate. He resembles the viper that ate my sister last year when she fell to the ground learning how to fly. He has the same disgusting manners and is just as slippery."

"Oh dear," responded the eel, appearing again. "It seems I have displeased you and I'm sorry for that, but you're being unfair to me. I'm only a fish, not related at all to the viper which devoured your unattached sister. We may resemble one another in our shapes and movements, but we eels have an exceptional ability to wiggle, and I'm significantly more slippery. People call me an eel, and I'm pleased to meet you."

"My mate is sitting on her eggs," said the reed-warbler. "She can't tolerate much excitement."

"Thank you, reed-warbler," said the eel. "I have no intention of being bossy, but since I travel a lot myself, just like you and your mate, I only meant to chat with you, hoping to share views on the comings and goings in the lake."

"You travel? Can you also fly?" asked the reed-warbler.

"Not exactly," replied the eel. "I can't fly, but I'm best at wiggling. I can even travel across land, which few fish can imitate. In wet grass I'm in my element, as much as in the water, and if you give me a passably decent ditch to cross, I'll never complain. I've just come from the ocean, and after I've eaten and fattened myself up here, I'll head out to sea again."

"That is impressive," said reed-warbler.

"Yes," said the eel modestly. "And since I've seen so much of the world, it's exactly why all this fussy worrying over the newborns in the lake here seems absurd to me."

"You're not very understanding, my fine eel," said the reed-warbler. "We can see that you have neither a mate nor young ones."

"Well," said the eel, making a lovely flip of its tail, "it's just how you like to see it. But this year I have contributed to the world somewhere around a million newborn eels."

"Goodness!" interrupted mother-to-be reed-warbler, thinking how tired she got after just a few eggs.

"Aren't you exaggerating?" exclaimed her astonished mate, trying not to show it.

"It's very possible," replied the eel. "It isn't easy to figure it out precisely when the numbers are so large. But it doesn't make so much difference. Take away half of that, if it will make you feel better."

"What does your conscience say about fathering such an enormous number of offspring?"

"I haven't spoken to my conscience about it," said the eel.

"How about your mate's role in all this?" asked mother-to-be reed-warbler.

"Um... I can't tell you because I've never seen her."

"You've never seen your mate?"

"Nope, haven't seen my young ones either. We fish don't take all this family stuff so seriously."

"Honestly, you are doing your fellow-fish an injustice with such talk. Just a moment ago, I saw with my own eyes, right underneath us, the stickleback fish building a nest for their young."

"Stickleback fish!" said the eel contemptuously. "I don't like stickleback fish; they poke you horribly in the throat. But that's another story. I ask you: What is a stickleback fish? I remember once being caught and was about to be skinned. I was young then, and the kitchen girl, who was about to stick a knife in me, said... 'Quite a stickleback fish!'"

"Was she about to skin you alive?" asked father-to-be reed-warbler. "How on earth did you get out of that?"

"Thanks to being so slippery, I slid out of the kitchen girl's grip," replied the eel. "Of course, the mistress wouldn't touch my slimy body. Then I slid into the laundry sink, through the drainpipe, out the gutter, into the ditch, etc. You have to wiggle."

"I should say so!" replied the mother-to-be reed-warbler, still astonished.

"You experience a little of everything," said the eel. "But returning to what we were talking about... we eels release our newborns far out into the ocean, and they take care of themselves. As we are world travelers, we know what life requires of them, so we cast them all out together, en masse—a million of them at a time, as I said before... oh, maybe I said a half million; I don't mean to exaggerate. Those newborn... they quickly grasp how to fend for themselves. That was my experience, and that's how I learned the advantages to wiggling."

"I just can't imagine all this," said mother-to-be reed-warbler.

"I'm sorry," said the eel. "Maybe my experiences are too distasteful for an expectant mother sitting on her eggs."

"I believe that youngsters are some of the nicest, sweetest creatures in nature," she declared. "We have to love them, whether they are our own or belong to others."

"You females! You're always right," said the eel at the same time he was devouring two spring-fly larvae and an unsuspecting earthworm. "But... am I mistaken, or did I see you recently dining on a larva which your mate brought to you?"

"A larva?"

"Yes, isn't a larva also a newborn?"

"Help me!" said mother-to-be reed-warbler, who then fainted, nearly falling out of the nest.

"You need to wiggle," said the eel, and disappeared.

The reed-warbler revived his mate with three fat flies, seven sweet songs, and a thump on the neck with his beak.

"You should show me some appreciation," he said when she came to. "See how well I keep you in food and serenade you. Think how some other males would treat you!"

"Believe me, I do," she replied.

Mother Crayfish

All the pretty mother birds were sitting on their eggs with serious expressions, while their mates were singing to them or out catching flies.

It was no different with the reed-warblers. But it couldn't be denied that the reed-warbler was sometimes feeling quite tired and grouchy. He was thinking how easy the male eels, frogs, and perches had it, along with all the others who lived in the lake. One evening, sitting by the nest, he sang to his tired mate for a while, trying to arouse some interest in her.

Now it's a wonderful springtime again,
Though it is tough for a little songster.

A week ago, I was making love,
But now I'm busy catching flies.

For my mate who sits on eggs we share,
In them, I hear lovely singing voices.

And when they emerge, they'll be so hungry,
But yes, I will be very happy too.

"If you're tired of all this effort, you shouldn't have started it," said the mother-to-be reed-warbler. "You tempted me in the beginning. You were so handsome... but now, I think you're losing some color."

"It's tough," he replied, "going out and searching for flies in all kinds of weather. It's more than I bargained for."

"I don't think you're singing nicely anymore," she said.

"Don't you think so? I can be silent; it's for your sake that I chirp. Oh, come on, mate... you know I'm only having a little fun. I'm looking forward to welcoming the nestlings. I am honored. And what a pleasure to stuff them until they burst. Probably just three is enough..."

"You should be ashamed of yourself," she responded.

"I am, dearest, over the two eggs so far, but since I don't know what those two are to become, it doesn't matter."

She made a serious face, and at the same moment he caught a fat fly on the wing and after putting it in her mouth, trilled a lovely tune so she fell in love with him all over again.

Then, an enormous sigh came out from the water under an overhang.

"That's coming from some mother," said the reed-warbler. "I can hear her clearly."

"It sure does," said a rough voice.

The reed-warblers peeked down and spied a crayfish sitting in the mud, staring with her eyes sticking out.

"Oh, is it you, crayfish?" asked the reed-warbler.

"Yes, it is I, little mother," said the crayfish... "myself, and no one else. I've been sitting here in the dirt listening to what the high and mighty ones were chatting about. Wow, how some elegant females can live it up compared to others, like me for example."

"Each to its own," replied the mother-to-be reed-warbler. "Believe me, it isn't much fun sitting here on these hard lumps, and sweating."

The crayfish looked cross-eyed and folded her antennae.

"Well, that's easy for you to say," she said. "How long does it take to brood your eggs? I guess about four to five weeks; it takes six months for mine."

"Well, but you can move around a bit, I suppose."

"You think so?" said the mother crayfish; "it's always a little hard to move for a crayfish. You have only five eggs, but I have two hundred."

"Wow!" replied the reed-warbler. "Your poor mate must work himself to the bone to provide food for such an enormous family."

"He... that monster!" replied the crayfish. "He looks after himself, all right. I haven't seen him since the one time we got together!"

"You must have an exceptionally large nest for all those eggs," responded the reed-warbler.

"Apparently, you are not familiar with the circumstances of us commoners, little mother," said the crayfish. "There isn't much help for our kind. No, honestly, I have to carry the eggs around with me all the time."

"But where do you keep them, crayfish?"

"I carry them on the underside of my legs. I have ten small rear legs besides the eight regular ones in the front, and then there are my claws to snatch at prey, which are necessary if I'm to have a chance in this rotten world. And on every one of those rear legs, there is a clump of twenty eggs. There are two hundred in all. You can see them if you like; the eggs are healthy."

With that, the crayfish turned over onto her back and straightened out her tail as much as she could. Sure enough, there were the eggs attached to ten small, black legs.

"That's what you get for having too many rear legs," joked the father-to-be reed-warbler.

"You should be ashamed of yourself making fun of this poor mother," said his mate.

"Oh, males think they're always so witty," said the crayfish sarcastically as she slowly turned over again. She looked up at the female reed-warbler in her nest and whispered: "We females understand each other better. I wouldn't mind all the eggs so much if only it didn't mean that I can't change when I'm carrying them."

"Change?" said the mother-to-be reed-warbler, perplexed.

"Yes, I know you molt once in a while. I've seen your feathers floating on the water. It is so easy with a feather here and a feather there, and soon it's all normal again. But when someone like me who has a stiff shell and must discard the entire thing at one time... now that's a problem. I can't do that when I have to walk around with the eggs. I only change once a year, but since I've mated, I'm stuck in this old shell and well... you start putting on some weight, and it's hard on me sometimes."

The reed-warbler and his mate looked at each other; this story deeply touched them. He sang to her because he was afraid that all the sadness would make the incubating eggs melancholy and harm the nestlings' singing voices. But they were also quite puzzled about a crayfish changing her shell. Then, all at once, the crayfish screamed out, kicking with her front claws, and behaving like she was mad.

"Look out! Here comes the monster!"

Mother-to-be reed-warbler leaned so far over the edge of the nest that she would have plopped into the lake if her mate hadn't given her a decent nudge. But he didn't have time to scold her because he was curious too, and so both of them stared down into the water and there he was... the crayfish's mate, slowly crawling backwards towards her.

"Hello, old mate," he said. "I'm ready for molting."

"Oh, really, you old beast!" she screamed. "That's just like you, showing up when it pleases you. You're always running around, doing whatever you want, while your poor, faithful mate is stuck with legs full of eggs. You should think more about me and the youngsters."

"Why should I, old mate?" he replied. "What good does it do for me to worry about that? And why should I meddle in a mother's work, anyway? What needs doing, just do it. Now keep quiet while I change my shell here. This changing isn't just fooling around; it's serious work."

The reed-warblers stared, open-beaked, as the male crayfish flipped himself on his back. Then, he raised himself up on his tail, and began tearing and shaking until the hard shell across his back started to come loose. He continued to bend and twist until he maneuvered the whole body-covering shell over his head, and he righted himself, standing there with a fresh new shell.

"Well, that's done," he said, puffing. "Now it's time to do the legs."

Reed-warbler looked momentarily away, but she quickly peeked down again. The crayfish shook and jerked, and… one-two-three… the shell of the tail was lying by itself. Now he was soft and strange to look at and talked with a low voice.

"So long, old mate, and say hello to the youngsters, because they'll have taken off while I'm gone for about ten days, and I won't be around to chat with anybody."

"You beast, you monster!" screamed his crayfish mate. "Just look… now he's crawling into his hole where he'll just lie there, vegetating and hardening his spanking new shell covering, enormously pleased with himself. Then off he goes, eating and drinking like a princeling."

She wrung her claws, and her eyes were almost popping out of her head.

"I could just crawl into the hole with him and squeeze him to death," she said. "His life isn't worth two cents seeing the condition he's in now. But I loved him once, and I'm just a hysterical female, so they say. Oh, how did I ever get involved with him!"

"Yes, yes, mother crayfish, but you have the young ones to think about," said the mother-to-be reed-warbler.

"Yes, I suppose," she answered, seeming to calm down. "They are almost my only consolation. Those sweet kids; I could just devour them. You must see how they'll hang on to me the first week, hovering around me and wanting cuddling."

"Isn't that lovely," said the mother-to-be reed-warbler.

"Yes, and they won't be any trouble afterwards. When they're only a week old, they go out into the big world and take care of themselves. It's in their nature. It's unheard of in the lake that a twelve-day-old crayfish has been a burden to its family. And then you're done with them, which can be sad, but it makes it easier, too. Can you imagine two hundred kids in a smaller household, like in your nest.? But you will see them when they arrive. I have to watch out I don't eat them, being as they are so adorable."

"But now I want to offer you something, crayfish," said the reed-warbler. "When mine break out of the eggs, you're going to get the shells!"

"Oh, how kind of you," said the crayfish. "After consuming them, those eggshells will give me lots of the calcium I need for my new, stiff exterior shell once my babies are here. You must promise to look in on them; they're so adorable."

Before the reed-warblers could reply, a large carp came by, looking tired and sad.

"You'll eat them yourself, you disgusting old witch" it said.

"Oh, I would never!" screamed crayfish and fled backwards into her hole and disappeared.

As the carp swam away with its tired, sad expression, the reed-warbler sat, open-beaked on his reed, and his mate fainted right on top of her five eggs.

The Water Spider

Reed-warbler was not feeling well. She was jittery, feverish, and tired of sitting on her eggs, and either she couldn't sleep at night, or she had dreams about the crayfish, the carp, and the eel, screaming out sometimes so that her mate almost fell into the lake from fright.

"I wish that we had settled in some other place," she said. "Here in the lake, there are only commoners around us. Remember how touched I was over the plight of the crayfish? Do you really think the crayfish eats her own young?"

Before he could answer, the eel stuck its head up from the mud, and in a humble voice said: "Without a doubt. She does if she can catch them. As soon as they can though, those newborns disappear quickly because they have an inkling of what awaits them. They're smarter than we think."

"That's terrible," said the reed-warbler.

"Well, yes," said the eel. "One consumes so much through the years, but I don't condemn her for it. It doesn't look very nice, right in the middle of... Oh, there's the pike! I have to run for cover," as the eel sped away.

✳   ✳   ✳

The pike was meandering among the reeds with a wide-open mouth showing a thousand sharp teeth and evil eyes.

"Go away, you horrible creature!" said mother-to-be reed-warbler.

"Come down here, ducky, and I'll eat you alive," said the pike, sneering with his teeth.

"Heaven forbid it! Go where you usually hang out," said the insulted reed-warbler.

"Why should I? I eat everything," said the pike... "EVERYTHING, but that's the way I've always been. I can smell the eel, I can smell the crayfish, and I can smell the carp. Where are they, you annoying bird? Tell me right away, or I'll knock your miserable nest off the reeds with a flick of my tail."

The reed-warblers remained silent out of fear, and the pike slammed its tail and swam away. The tail strike was so powerful that the reeds gasped and swayed, and the reed-warblers flew into the air with fearful cries.

But the reeds held, and the nest remained hanging. The reed-warbler came back to sit on her eggs again, and when her mate returned, he serenaded her to help her get over how terrified she had been. It had been a terrible experience, but now they could rest.

"It's very comfortable here," she said finally.

"You're taking this too personally," her mate said. "Life is the same everywhere, and if only we enjoy each other, let us be content. I'm much more concerned that all the surrounding excitement will injure the voices of our young ones, so they'll shame us at the autumn concert. Pull yourself together and you'll be fine."

"You sure know how to talk," she replied. "I know what life is all about. A viper ate my innocent sister, and a hawk took my mother just after she had taught us how to fly. Last year in the fall, I had to flee quickly to Italy if I would not starve to death. Then you came into my life, and I learned that settling down is not the simple bliss one hears about. While I'd like a peaceful environment since I'm expecting, I can only wonder about how the nestlings will thrive in this murder-pit we live in. Youngsters take their lead from others, and what an example they'll get here! It could get even worse; they could end up with them eating their parents!"

"Sure, why not if they taste good?" said a quiet voice down at the water's edge.

The mother-to-be reed-warbler became startled at that, fearing to look down, but there, sitting on a waterlily pad, was a small water spider polishing her fine velvety coat.

"You're looking so crossly at me, but you mustn't eat me," the water spider said to the reed-warbler's mate. "I'll be heavy in your stomach and I'm also poisonous... useful in housekeeping chores. Otherwise, you'll find I'm one of the most good-natured females around here."

"But didn't you say that it's all right to eat your parents?" questioned the mother-to-be reed-warbler.

"Possibly for a bird, I spoke a bit too frankly," said the water spider. "What passes as reasonable for one species, makes little sense for another. All I recall is that I ate my mother last year, and she was a fine, fat old female."

"Sing to me, or I will die," screamed the mother-to-be reed-warbler.

So, her mate sighed and then sang to her. Meanwhile, they both peeked down at the water spider and watched as she sprang into the water submerging her head. A moment later, she let her abdomen position itself over the surface of the water, allowing web-like threads to ooze out of her until they filled up with air. Then the animal sank, glistening like silver as she glided toward the bottom.

"That's a pretty sight," said the reed-warbler.

"Be quiet," said his mate, staring down so hard she almost stretched her neck off and nearly fell out of the nest again.

Deep down in a bush that hung over the water's edge, the water spider had spun a dome-shaped object that immediately filled up with air from the passing breeze. The dome was of the finest webbing, tethered on all sides with strong, fine threads so it couldn't blow away. And surrounding the dome, almost touching the water, was a bigger web structure for capturing prey like the water mite that had just bumped into it. The spider shot out of the water, pulled the mite into the dome, and set about her meal.

"That's weird; she has a nest, something like ours, hanging up above the water in the reeds," said the mother-to-be reed-warbler. "I wonder if she also sits on her eggs like I do?"

"Ask her," father-to-be reed-warbler replied.

"First, I want to know more about this business with her mother; can you believe that?" she said firmly.

Later, the water spider came by again, sitting on the waterlily as she groomed herself.

"Were you spying on me taking a meal?" she asked. "I'm settled here; I have a peaceful life and a lovely home. While I'm an animal that lives above ground, just like you, my business is in the water, so I've arranged things for myself in the simplest way I could. Believe me, it's very comfortable down there. In the winter, I close myself in and take a very long snooze."

"Don't you brood eggs?" asked reed-warbler.

"Well... yes," she replied. "I have everything that belongs to a proper household. I have lots of eggs, and as I lay them, I hang them up in bundles at the top of my dome."

"Don't you sit on them?" asked the mother-to-be reed warbler.

"No, my dear. That much of a warm heart, I don't have. Nor is it necessary. They'll hatch out by themselves."

"Did your mate help you build the dome?" inquired mother-to-be reed-warbler.

"He had plenty to do building for himself, the poor wretch," she said. "Please don't think I'd ever allow him into my private space He made a little place for himself next door, with a tunnel between us, and that was more than sufficient."

"Was?" asked reed-warbler. "Isn't he there anymore? Please don't hold it against me for all these questions. I have such a hard time understanding the mating customs of all you commoners. Do you have any idea where your mate is now?"

"Oh, of course I know where he is," replied the water spider. "Well, almost. Because I ate him on Wednesday."

"Spare me!" said mother-to-be reed-warbler, as she nearly fainted.

"He was constantly in the way, and I didn't know what to do with him. So, I ate him, and what a tough fellow he was."

"On Wednesday you ate your mate, and last year you ate your mother," said reed-warbler. "Sing for me, mate," she screamed, "or that horrible female will murder me."

But her mate was so shocked also that he couldn't utter a sound. The water spider, listening in, felt nothing at all.

"Oh, listen now, mother reed-warbler," the water spider responded. "It was only because of hunger, and when my mother, err... left us, I wasn't the only one in need; my brothers and sisters were starving too, and there wasn't anything else edible as it was late in the fall. Our mother came strolling along, and so we ate her."

With that, the water spider jumped into the water again, but the reed-warbler was in a worse shape and didn't get her forty winks of sleep. She kept constantly whispering to herself: "She ate her mother, and then she ate her mate, too, on Wednesday..."

"Don't think about it anymore," replied her mate. "The hawk got your mother, and if you eat me, I know it will be out of love."

"Shame on you for joking at times like this," she replied sternly. "Just sing to me."

"I'm sure the 'times', as you say, are all the same, but it's always the time you're in now that is the worst." So, as morning came, and the sun appeared, he sang to his little brown mate, which made her happy again. For a while.

The Bladderwort

As mother-to-be reed-warbler neared her due date, there was no end to her nervousness and complaining. Nothing her mate did satisfied her. If he brought her a fly, she shook her head at him and asked how he could imagine that she could eat anything in view of the imminent arrival of the most important event in her life. If he didn't bring her anything, she accused him of intending to starve her to death. If he sang to her, she couldn't stand to listen. If he was silent, it was obvious he didn't care for her anymore.

"You're not really being very fair to me," he said. "You should try living with an eel or a crayfish, and then you'd see."

"If you had taken the water spider for a mate," she said, "you'd have been eaten!"

"Mother reed-warbler! I'm back, my friend!" yelled the crayfish from the mud.

"So? What do you want?" she asked grumpily.

"I'd just like to remind you not to forget me... will you remember the eggshells?"

"I won't have the slightest thing to do with such a vile animal who'd eat her own newborns," said the mother-to-be reed-warbler.

∗   ∗   ∗

"Don't bother with that nasty carp who was here the other day," said the crayfish, changing the subject. "Such a horrible fellow; he doesn't even belong in the lake. Quite an animal, for sure. Some humans have put him in here, allowing him to grow, so they can eat him later. See how large and fat he's become; people keep feeding him. He has time on his hands, not needing to find his own meals; he just swims around slandering and mocking the poor and depriving them of any pity from the better-offs."

"Will you shut up, crayfish," said the father-to-be reed-warbler. "You're driving my mate crazy with your drivel."

24

"I'm so sorry; I only wanted to remind you about the shells," said the crayfish sulkily and crawled backwards into her hole.

"Why are you always thinking so hard about that riffraff," said the reed-warbler to his mate. "There's more to this world than crayfish, eels, and water spiders. Find something beautiful to look at. It will be good for your morale."

"Show me something," she replied unenthusiastically.

"Look at that beautiful, white flower lying just below us," he said. "See how it lifts itself out of the water to brighten our day. It's neither a thief nor a bandit."

It really was a lovely white flower that had grown up from the bottom on a long, thin stem, and exhibited exceptional sweetness and innocence. Mother-to-be reed-warbler looked at it affectionately, and her mood improved.

"What's your name, sweet flower," she asked. "Can I look at you awhile?"

"That's okay," the flower answered. "I'm called a bladderwort. I know I'm beautiful, but other plants look down upon me because I'm a strange carnivore that eats and digests insects and other vermin. Anyway, I don't have time to talk to you; I need to go about my business."

Reed-warbler stretched her neck and looked down into the water.

"That disgusting water spider has her nest among the bladderwort leaves," she said.

"So what? There's nothing the bladderwort can do about that," responded her mate. "That's what being a flower is all about, fixed in place and accept whatever comes to them quietly, while sucking up nourishment from the ground. The bladderworts don't have any spots on their flowers nor blood in their leaves, and when their flowers arrive, it makes them seem so delicate and poetic, I think…"

"Be quiet," she interrupted. "They're talking together."

Both of the reed-warblers leaned down and listened.

*   *   *

"Did you catch anything?" asked the bladderwort.

"Sure," replied the water spider. "I'm not turning in without eating something. At this time of the year, there are lots of water mites, so I'm not complaining. How is it going with you?"

"Great, thank you," said the bladderwort. "I've devoured one hundred and fifty ant larvae and forty carp fry this afternoon. But I'm still hungry; I don't really think I can ever be full."

"What is she talking about?" whispered mother-to-be reed-warbler, looking terrified at her mate.

"Keep quiet," he replied. "Let's hear more about this."

The water spider went into her chamber, hung up seven eggs, took a mouthful of air, and came out again.

"You're really a horrible thief," the water spider said to the bladderwort. "If I wasn't taking lodging from you, I'd get quite upset. You take prey right out of my mouth."

"What rubbish," said the bladderwort. "There's enough for both of us. I'm thrilled that I have a lodger who's in the same business as I am. That way, we have something to chat about."

"It's downright puzzling that a stationary flower like you eats like a creature that moves about like a common thief," said the water spider. "It's not something one expects from your kind."

"What am I supposed to say to that?" asked the bladderwort. "Times are hard; there are a lot of us, and the ground is lacking nutrients. We have to eat what's available. That's when I came up with this strategy, and it works really well. But I also have my machinery in order. Do you want to see how I do it?"

"I'd like that," said the water spider. "But promise you won't hurt me... okay?"

"Relax," said the bladderwort chuckling. "You're too large for me. Run along one of my stems, and I'll explain the entire thing to you."

The water spider walked a brief stretch, slipping down to a branch, and stopped to look at a little bladder resembling a small pod resting there.

"That's one of my traps," said the bladderwort. "I have a couple hundred of them to catch prey in."

"Can you eat a couple hundred water mites at one time?" said the water spider enviously.

"I could if they would come. But I'm never that lucky. Do you want to see it? On the side of the bladder is a little flap which is loose. When some fool prey runs into it, it collapses, the bladders close, and whoops! ... the poor wretch falls into the bladder. He can't come out, and then I digest him at my leisure. You must watch closely though, because I'm super-fast when I snag my victims."

"Did you hear that?" whispered reed-warbler.

"Yes," her mate replied, looking very serious.

The water spider couldn't resist poking at the bladderwort's flap with one of her legs.

"Ouch!" she screamed suddenly and lurched backwards with a start, but her leg remained in the bladder. Instantly, the leg disappeared completely into the bladder and the flap closed.

"Can I have my leg back?" the water spider said angrily.

"Do I have your leg?" asked the bladderwort. "Well, you must have been too near the flap. What can I say, my friend, didn't I warn you?"

"You said I was too big."

"Well, you are too big–unfortunately–but I can enjoy eating my prey a bit at a time."

"That's not very nice of you since you are my host," said the water spider. "But as I have seven other legs, I will forgive you."

"Please do, my friend!" said the bladderwort. "You need to understand that I'm not completely in control of myself when someone messes with my flap. I just have to eat whatever falls inside. Keep your eye out."

"Not to worry," said the water spider. "A sneak like you needs watching carefully. Would it be indiscreet of me to ask how my leg tastes?"

"Oh," said the bladderwort. "There wasn't much to it; I'm all done with digesting it already. Please have a look at what's left."

And immediately the flap opened up, and a little tiny fragment fell into the water.

"Is that my leg?" inquired the water spider.

"Don't you recognize it?"

The water spider stood back and looked at the stump as the bladderwort laughed.

"Good night," muttered the water spider and limped dejectedly back into her chamber.

"Good night," said the bladderwort nicely."Have a nice hunt tomorrow."

"Will someone tell me I'm imagining this!" said mother-to-be reed-warbler. "I'll never get over this."

But then she noticed something moving under her.

*　*　*

"The newborns!" she screamed, and in a flash, she was on the edge of the nest, and on the other side, her mate looked down anxiously.

One egg had broken completely in two, and another was cracking. There lay a little tiny blind and naked newborn in the nest, and the cutest little leg was sticking out of the other egg.

"Have you ever seen the likes of it!" she yelled. "Isn't it lovely?"

"Beautiful!" he responded.

They then pecked at the other eggs carefully while, from inside, the tiny newborns also tapped away with their little beaks. A few minutes later, all five of them were free of their eggshells.

"Help me clean up," she demanded of the new father. And from all directions, the shells flew out from the nest into the water.

"Blessings on you," called the crayfish from down below while she was out on her evening stroll, but no one in the nest heard her.

The reed-warblers were besides themselves with joy and were not thinking of anything else. Mother reed-warbler even forgot to keep the hatchlings warm.

"Why aren't you sitting on them? Are you crazy?" her mate demanded, "they'll freeze to death."

Obediently, she gently sat on them, covering them up against the cold, and staring at them at every chance. Father reed-warbler perched on top of a reed for half the night and sang to his new family.

The Mayfly

The entire lake was alive. Besides the big awful pikes, the large, good-natured carps, the roach fish and the perch, the stick-lebacks and eels, there were also crayfish and frogs, salamanders, swamp snails, and freshwater clams, water-beetles, daddy-long-legs, whirlpools, and many other creatures.

A mother duck was quacking at her ducklings, a swan glided over the water with a bent neck and spreading wings, so elegant and lovely. A dragonfly buzzed in the air, her young ones creeping along the surface of the water, eating until they were fit to burst. But it didn't matter; it was almost normal to burst before they amounted to anything.

There was the bladderwort with its innocent white flowers floating on the water and with a stranglehold down at the bottom but still sharing space with the water spider who now had the whole of her chamber filled with eggs. A hundred thousand gnat larvae lay on top of the water, sticking their breathing tubes into the air, ever watchful for even a shadow on the water which would send them rushing to the bottom. The same number of mosquitoes danced in the air, while the lovely vain waterlily, knowing how beautiful it was, kept its distance.

There were an umpteen number of lively tadpoles, and if you took just a drop of water and examined it under a magnifying glass, you'd see numerous tiny little animals squirming around and eating each other without so much as a thought.

But just under the nest of the reed-warblers, a mayfly larva was beside herself with anxiety. She had spoken to mother reed-warbler one day when she had ventured down the reeds in search of more food for her five babies who never had enough to eat and were constantly demanding more. The mayfly larva had just surfaced, and the reed-warbler's bill was there, waiting.

"Oh please, let me live," said the mayfly larva.

"You say that," said reed-warbler, "but my babies also need to live."

She was about to snatch it up, but the mayfly larva wiggled so much and seemed so distraught, that she didn't have the heart.

"Just listen to me for a second," said the larva, "and then I'm confident you won't harm me. I'm so tiny and thin and will hardly take up any room in you or your nestlings' stomachs."

"So, what is it?" asked mother reed-warbler.

"I just live here for a while as I slowly grow bigger," explained the larva. "I've heard how you chat with your mate, with the crayfish, the eel, and the spider. You said such pleasant things to them. I'm certain you have a good heart."

"I don't know about my heart," replied the reed-warbler, "but I have five hungry nestlings."

"But, I'm a newborn also," begged the larva, "and I want so much to live until I'm able to complete my life cycle."

"Do you really think life is so great?" responded the reed-warbler.

"I don't know about that. I'm still a larva, just creeping around and waiting. When I'm grown up, I'll get wings and shall be able to fly about just like you."

"Do you fancy yourself a bird?" said reed-warbler.

"Oh, no. I'm not aiming so high. I'm just happy to be a spring mayfly."

"I'm familiar with your type; I have eaten a lot of you; you're delicious," replied reed-warbler.

"Well, don't eat me now, but at least wait until I've grown up, and flew around for a while. Please? You understand that I only live a few hours after I've gotten my wings. I'll have just enough time to fly around the lake once, lay my eggs in the water, and then I will die. That's the time to eat me. But let me live now, and please tell that to your mate too, because he chased me two times."

The reed-warbler considered this for a moment, her beak still poised, but becoming a mother had improved her mood.

"Oh, go on then," said reed-warbler, "It's probably dumb of me since you could be lying, and someone else will consume you before long."

"I'll try my best to avoid that," said the larva. "But, I'm so grateful."

When the reed-warbler returned to the nest with six gnat larva she had caught in her bill, her mate was also there with a dragonfly which the nestlings had torn to pieces and were devouring with delirious screeching.

"They don't lack for an appetite, nor a voice for yelling either," he said. "I only hope they can start fending for themselves. I'm looking like a skeleton."

"And what about me?" said his mate, adding, "but the kids are thriving and that's the most important thing."

He sighed, flew away, came back, flew away again, and that's how it went until evening. Then they sat on the edge of the nest, exhausted, and gazed out over the shining lake.

"It's strange how much life's daily routines demand from you," she said. "Sometimes I'm so tired that I can understand those animals that let their kids fend for themselves. Did you notice the eel the other day, how fat and happy he was?"

"Are you talking about me again?" interjected the eel, sticking his head up from the deep.

"Is it you again, eel? You seem to be everywhere," said mother reed-warbler.

"Pretty much. Keep wiggling," replied the eel.

"Have you heard anything from your youngsters?"

"No, thank goodness. They're as thin as threads to begin with, but later they'll have their fling in the saltwater and have a splendid time, as long as they don't end up as prey for some predator. But some are sure to survive, and you'll see them one day come wiggling in just like I did as they sense that there's something interesting here. They won't mind swimming an extra couple miles."

"Oh, I see," said mother reed-warbler.

"Do you groan and ache from the youngsters' mischief?" inquired the eel. "Didn't I tell you to expect that?"

"Not really," she replied. "I'd never behave like you do. We all have responsibilities, and the higher on nature's pecking order you are, the greater are the tasks that face us."

"Thank goodness I'm low in rank then," said the eel. "I'm perfectly happy living in the muck."

"But you know," responded father reed-warbler, "while I realize that there is some goodness in nature, let's also admit there's lots of nonsense and nastiness in the world. So, it's important that we animals of superior rank constantly apply ourselves; we strive to higher expectations. The most ideal state in nature is a father working for the good of his family, even if it gets demanding sometimes."

"It's quite something to see you being so high and mighty today, reed-warbler," said the eel. "Each to its own, but I must confess I've not experienced much of the outstanding things in life. I have wiggled my way around many places in the world; it seems like it's just eat, eat, and eat some more... everywhere. However, I still say those folks taking care of youngsters are the worst of all. I'm off now. Bye!"

"Such a horrible creature when we were good enough to tell him what's important in life," said mother reed-warbler. "But I agree completely with you, mate. I did something kindly today. Follow me."

She led her mate down the reeds and peeked into the water.

"Are you there my little day-old larva?" she asked.

"Yes, thanks," replied the mayfly larva.

"And you're doing fine?"

"Oh, yes. The eel almost got me, and I almost fell into the bladderwort trap, and before that, the water spider was out after me. Otherwise, everything is great."

"What's this all about?" inquired her mate.

"Well," answered mother reed-warbler, "I have a protégé here. A little, day-old mayfly larva, and I promised not to eat her because she is so looking forward to growing up, even though she'll only then live a couple of hours, the poor thing."

Reed-warbler said nothing about eating her when she was fully grown, which made her mate angry.

"What sentimental nonsense," her mate replied. "Do you really think you're acting like a responsible mother with five nestlings to feed? How dumb!"

"I think it was decent of me; let her live," insisted mother reed- warbler.

"Ridiculous!" screamed her mate. "Decency has nothing to do with capturing prey for food, or otherwise we'll all die of starvation. It doesn't matter that she's such a lower order creature."

He ran down the reed and looked around for the mayfly larva to eat her, but the larva heard what the reed-warbler said and scurried down to the bottom of the lake, her whole-body trembling.

The Carp

Summer passed and things got worse, and also busier. All the newborns in the world had come out of their eggs, crowding the waters of the lake. Way out in the middle, it was green with millions of dead and rotting algae that stank so badly that seven large perches died of the smell and floated into the shore with their bellies in the air.

"The lake is blossoming," said the rushes sarcastically.

"There a disgusting odor here at the lake," said mother reed-warbler

"I think it's nice here," said the carp who didn't have a sense of smell.

The carp swam between the reeds where it had discovered a recent friend living in them, a freshwater clam which plowed its narrow way through the muck or attached itself to the bottom and yawned. These two got along well because they were steady and quiet fellows who lived in similar ways.

"I don't feel like going on a wild chase after prey anymore," said the carp. "I open up my mouth where the water is a bit thick and let run in whatever there is. There's always something hanging around. Then I'm free from having to kill and I don't have to see and experience all the misery."

"Just like with us clams; I use exactly the same method. It's more elegant, and I've gotten fat from it."

The two of them chatted some more, yawning the entire time but still enjoying themselves immensely.

"Make sure you don't get too close to them," said mother reed-warbler to the mayfly larva.

"Yes, thanks for the advice," said the mayfly larva.

"The carp and the clams are nicer than the others," said reed-warbler to her mate.

"Yes, but why is that?" said the eel that was always around when you were least thinking about him. "They do the same things we do, except the animals they eat are much smaller than they are."

"There is a difference," said father reed-warbler. "Your lower ranking doesn't let you see it."

"Yes, but you need to wiggle," said the eel from force of habit.

Father reed-warbler thought better of responding, but turned to the carp and the clam, piped a little trill, and said politely: "My mate and I bring you greetings. We have observed with pleasure how much finer you conduct your lives than most of the lake's other inhabitants."

"We have suffered a lot at the sight of the enormous brutality..." he paused a moment, snapping at a blowfly, and throwing it into the nest to the young. "... which takes place in this lake. It must be distasteful for smart, cultured lake-dwellers like you two to observe the undisguised, cynical crudeness by which they satisfy their..." he quickly snapped up a spring fly, consumed it, dried his bill, and continued ... "bodily needs". You two are different. If you had wings, I might have believed that originally you didn't belong at all to the group that calls this home."

"You're right," answered the carp and fluttered his fins courteously.

"Indeed," said the clam after yawning politely.

"I was born in another lake," related the carp. "But I must confess I don't have a clear recollection of it. I only know that the wild, bandit-like existence here didn't occur there. I don't believe there were any other fish but carps in the lake which made the environs easier to live in. It was a proud carp pond. They fed us five times a day, and they removed everything that might irritate us. We never saw such things as you have here: pikes, water-spiders, and those horrible bladderworts."

"It must have been idyllic," said father reed-warbler. "May I ask: Were there any reed-warblers around?"

"Yes," said the carp. "I believe they had permission to build in the reeds. Also, there were several frogs present, presumably there to cheer us up with their croaking."

"How did you get here?"

"Well," said the carp. "I don't know how to answer that. I mean, we came here in a large bucket, I and many companions, and they spilled us out into this lake. I can't think of any other reason except to improve the environs here. We had nothing to complain about where we were. Have you heard about the smart, cultured humans in these parts proposing such an idea?"

"No," said father reed-warbler. "It never happened as long as I can remember, but I've only been here since spring."

"Oh, I see," said the carp. "I've been here four years, but I wish I were somewhere else. There's the pike that constantly terrorizes us. Many of my fellow-carp have disappeared mysteriously, and honestly, I think the pike has eaten them. As you rightly say, this is an uncivilized place. Maybe you've already noticed it. But you're fairly lucky. You'll be leaving in the fall I suppose?"

"Yes, a brief excursion to Italy," said reed-warbler. "With the family."

The carp treaded in place a bit and pondered. Then it yawned a couple of times and said: "Maybe you can do me a favor. I thought of it after seeing your marvelously pointed bill."

"My pleasure," said father reed-warbler.

"See, everyone has his cross to bear, and mine is in my gills. Would you look?"

The carp opened the covers of his gills and the reed-warbler ran down the reed to peek in.

"Well, imagine that!" said the reed-warbler. "There something in there that has the shape of a cross."

"That's a parasite," said the carp, sighing.

"What's that?" responded the reed-warbler.

"The parasite? ... yes, I've had that with me ever since I swam in that other marvelous carp pond I told you about. Even then it hurt a lot, but lately I can barely stand it. You may know that the parasite originally consisted of two worms, the kind that don't like to work themselves, but take up lodging somewhere and feed on their hosts. I have about twenty of them in my stomach, but they don't bother me nearly so much as the one in my gills. To be even meaner, these rascals have the habit of lying on each other crosswise. They adhere to each other until they are mature, and then they eat away at me with their combined strength."

"I've heard nothing like that," said the reed-warbler.

"In the same way, I have another parasite in the gill on the other side of my head," said the carp. "We can chat about that later. Now, I'd ask you to seize the beast with your bill. I'll be so grateful as it hurts me so much; I'd rather die than live any longer like this."

The reed-warbler was just about to lean forward and prod his beak into the carp gills when, all at once, it seemed as if the world was ending.

The stand of reeds heaved, the reeds themselves cracked, the reed-warblers screamed, the carp splashed furiously; the clams turn over, and the water spider's chamber was crushed.

"At last!" resounded the voice of the pike.

"Spare me! Spare me!" screamed the carp.

What happened there at that spot, no one has ever said exactly.

With that, the pike emerged from the reeds as the carp thrashed about between the pike jaws, his teeth digging in further and further. Everyone nearby tried to cover their eyes or turn away, expecting to die, when it slowly got quiet again. When the reed-warblers and other creatures had recovered, the pike had left, and only the fin tail of the carp remained, floating on the surface of the water.

The reed-warblers' nest was flopping down on one side, and they needed to work awhile to repair it. Otherwise, the youngsters were fine, and they shortly got over their fright. The water cleared up again, and the clam sat below, yawning.

"That was a noble creature, your friend that departed," said father reed-warbler.

"Yes," replied the clam. "Did you know I experienced something similar?"

"We look forward to hearing your story tomorrow," responded reed-warbler. "Today we're just too shaken to stand any more discussion."

And with that the carp fin tail sank to the bottom, but it only got as far as the crayfish who seized it and hauled it into her hole.

"Poor creatures must be happy with the things the higher orders throw away," she said.

The Clam

The next evening, father reed-warbler peeked down into the water. The freshwater clam was sitting there, yawning as usual, unaffected by the sudden loss of the carp.

"Good evening," said the reed-warbler. "How are you managing after your friend's unfortunate departure?"

"Well, thanks for asking," said the clam. "It hasn't bothered me much. But nothing really bothers me very much. It's only when you stick something in between my shells I get mad, squeeze hard, and then close up."

"I would do that in your place, too," responded the reed-warbler. "Your level-headedness is enviable, but I think your close companion's loss..."

"I'm not cozy with anyone, and the carp was not my close companion," interrupted the clam. "We didn't compete so we could easily spend time together. The carp's manner of speaking often amused me, but I never contradict anyone unless one tries to stick something between my shells. The carp had some business with humans, and I'm not one for that. Some animals become strange, like you are... somewhat."

"I'll take that as a compliment," said the father reed-warbler, who seemed slightly insulted but didn't let on. "I have nothing to do with humans either, except they protect me, and because of my lovely songs, they don't have the heart to hurt me. Whenever they encounter me, they stop and listen. Many poets have written lovely verses about me."

"Have they?" said the clam. "They've done that for me too, but whatever they said, it was a pack of lies."

"Why? What did they say?"

"Oh, some drivel about pearls."

"My goodness, you have pearls?" exclaimed the reed-warbler. "Mate! Mate! The clam has pearls!"

"Absolutely not!" replied the clam immediately. "And stop screaming; one can hear it all over the lake. If anyone heard you, I'd risk being caught like a fish. There are no pearls coming from me, thank goodness."

"Ooh..." said father reed-warbler, feeling rather disappointed.

"It's just those poets that prattle on about pearls They gossip about how happy the clam is over the precious pearls we guard, and more. Do you even know what a pearl is?"

"No," admitted father reed-warbler.

"It's a disgusting, insolent parasite, something resembling the same nasty beggar which caused the carp so much pain. When it grows inside us, it hurts, so most of us get rid of it as soon as possible. We secrete the mother-of-pearl over it—that's a glassy-like substance—to ease the pain until the beast gives up and dies."

"Well... you learn something new every day," said the reed-warbler to his mate. How did we get so much nonsense in our heads? Soon, there won't be anything to believe in around here."

"Never mind. As long as we have our five gluttonous youngsters, it will never be empty and quiet here," she responded. "Hear that? They're already screaming for more."

"They'll get no more today," her mate replied in a disgruntled voice. "We've both been flying around for them all day long, and now I will take some time off... go have a chat with the neighbors. Give the nestlings some shreds of something to keep the peace."

The youngsters got the shreds, but they screamed out for more. But then, tiring of that, they fell asleep.

*　　*　　*

"Hello, clam. You hinted last night that you weren't born and raised here at the lake," said father reed-warbler. "So, where are you from?"

"Thanks for asking. I enjoy a chat in the evening, but nobody believes that you've experienced anything when you drift around slowly and you're low in rank. Well now, the story is..." began the clam, but then stopped abruptly. "Oh, wait! There's that rude creature, but I have to chat with her... please don't go away."

The reed-warbler looked down into the water, and there was the crayfish, busily adjusting her legs. She had crawled closer to the clam and was touching its shell with her legs. Seizing the chance, the clam slammed the shell shut on one of crayfish's legs, clipping it right through in the middle. The crayfish screamed and beat on the clam with her claws, but the only laughter came from inside the clam's shell.

"What a jerk you are, clam!" said the crayfish. "Can't you leave a working mother alone in peace?"

"Of course, I can," said the clam, "but why are you trying to pry into me? Why can't you leave me alone?"

"He's such a wretched clam!" screamed the crayfish, looking up at the reed-warbler. "A typical nasty mollusk! He's much lower in rank than I am, and still he's rude and nasty. I have twenty-one pairs of appendages on my body, many of which are legs; how many does he have?"

"That's twenty and a half pairs now," said the clam, laughing loudly.

The crayfish continued to quarrel and say horrible things about the clam, so the reed-warbler got annoyed with her too. "Stop your crude remarks," he said. "It has nothing to do with legs. I only have two."

"Heavens," said the crayfish. "With respect, reed-warbler, I know my place, but I don't understand how a fine male specimen like yourself would talk with such a lowlife mollusk like him."

Banging and scolding, crayfish retreated to her hole, letting her head and claws stick out. The clam opened up his shell again, but let four or five of his eyes, which sat on the rim of the shell, remain fixed on the crayfish. As soon as she moved even a little, he closed immediately.

"I have to be careful," said clam. "We show the world our hard, outer shell, but we are soft on the inside."

"I can see that," said the reed-warbler, "but you were about to tell me where you're from."

*   *   *

"Oh, well... yes. I was born in another lake far away," said the clam. "I can't give you a more detailed description of it; understandably in my position, you have little opportunity to look around. To be frank, it was about the same as it is here, with a vast number of lowlifes of all kinds, but there were a lot of clams. They sat in the mud as close together as sand grains on a bank and took the prey out of each other's mouths. If you took even a mouthful of water, it was ordinarily just an empty spray with nothing in it to eat, because someone else had already sucked it clean."

"So, what did you do then?" inquired the reed-warbler.

"I did nothing," replied the clam. "I start nothing unless someone sticks something into my shell. Then I get mad and close up."

"Oh, there you are, going on about that crayfish again? Do you have a little leg that you'd like amputated?"

"You talk like a dummy!" said the crayfish.

"But, getting back to my question... didn't you risk dying of hunger?" asked the reed-warbler.

"We don't die that easily," replied the clam, "We'll usually survive as long as we avoid an accident like the one the blessed carp experienced."

✳   ✳   ✳

"Did you know, I once spent an entire year in a room up on a human's table."

"Really?" said the reed-warbler. "How did you get up there?"

"It was a student or somebody who fished me up from the lake. He wrapped me in a piece of paper and laid me on the table. I believe he wanted to see how long I would live. Every Saturday, he

46

unwrapped me, threw a little more water on me, covered me again, and put me back up on the table. And I never died."

"But how did you escape?"

"Understand, while I was captive, other humans would come now and then to visit him, and they had to look, naturally, at the strange clam that wouldn't die. Among them was a young female who got furious with him for torturing me. He only laughed at her. After I had lain there for a year, he got very close to her. (Humans have this thing called engagement and marriage for finding and securing a mate). Anyway, they liked to snuggle up on the sofa next to me, and well... who knows what they were doing? But I wasn't so inconvenienced that I couldn't open up the shells a little and peek out to look at them. These humans, they sure are a strange bunch in how they get together!"

"Afterwards, he asked her if there wasn't something more that she wanted on this glorious day. Yeah, there was; she wanted him to throw me back into the water again. He laughed at her, but then they both took me immediately to the same lake where he fished me out and threw me in. So, I joined up with my old comrades again and started over."

"Yes, it's love," said the reed-warbler, looking tenderly at his mate.

"It's sweet love," she replied, giving him the eye again.

"I haven't anything against 'love', as you call it," added the clam, "but I know nothing about it from personal experience, either."

"I see," said the mother reed-warbler, "but don't you have a mate? Aren't you a female?"

"I'm neither male nor female. I'm just a giant clam, but when I act like a female—it varies—I lay my eggs, and that's all. Others in my family have definite mates, but not me."

"Are you good at taking care of your offspring?" inquired the reed-warbler.

"Not really," replied the clam. "My newborns are curious creatures and they just swim away as soon as they come out of the egg, moving around against wind and wave. When they are older, assuming they survive being eaten, they settle down and form shells with a lifestyle like mine."

"That's impressive, but let's not talk about the youngsters," said father reed-warbler... "it always makes my mate nervous. Tell us how you ended up in this lake."

"It's about a behavior instinct I have of getting furious when someone sticks something into my shell. I don't know if I told you about this property?"

"Several times," replied the reed-warbler. "I'll never forget it and will be careful."

"Just bear that in mind," said the clam. "Anyway, it was one of your kind that brought me here."

"A reed-warbler?"

"I don't know for sure if it was a reed-warbler; I don't see well out of the water."

"However, for me, one bird is as good as another. It was a seagull, probably. I was at the bottom, yawning as I usually do, and just above me was a little common roach fish. Suddenly, flash, plop and there was the gull, striking at the fish, but the gull was moving so fast that it descended quickly to the lake bottom, its complete body submerged in the water. One of the gull's small claws got entangled between my shells, and I closed up. The gull surfaced with the roach fish in his beak. He tore at me as I dangled from his hind claw and shook me terribly. But when I get mad, I also get powerfully strong and I held tight. In one sense the gull was the stronger of us, because it finally tore me loose, and rose through the water, and went aloft, carrying me along."

"What an amazing adventure," said the reed-warbler.

"We flew a respectful distance, high over fields and woods," continued the clam. "I could just peek out because the shells were slightly ajar on account of his claws. He dropped the fish, but I held on regardless of how hard the gull jerked and kicked. I had no intention of hanging on forever and I eventually saw this lake and let go, landing with a splash before I sunk to the bottom. I've been here ever since."

"Are you satisfied?"

"For the moment, yes. I have seen no other clams here, so it is significantly more comfortable than at the other place."

"That's a strange story," said father reed-warbler, and he then remained sitting, ever more thoughtful as night came on.

But his mate ran down the reed and peeked into the dark water.

"Are you there, my little larva?" she asked.

"Yes, thanks," said the mayfly larva.

"Did you have an enjoyable day?"

"Yes, thank you. The perch almost ate me, and then a duckling went after me. Later, a horrible dragon-fly larva and a water beetle chased me. Otherwise it went fine."

The Waterlily

"Don't you think we can let the young ones out soon?" asked father reed-warbler.

"Oh, heavens, no," said his mate. "It's completely out of the question that these sweet little things can stand on their own legs before the first month has gone by." They're stepping all over each other when I return with a measly fly. Listen, it's beginning to get a little difficult to find food. There are so many of us now with youngsters everywhere we turn, and they're all screaming for food."

"Are you beginning to experience what I told you was coming?" said the eel, sticking his head up from the mud.

"Be quiet and mind your own business, you nasty fish."

"But your mate has agreed with me for a long time," said the eel. "I can see it on his face. He'd give anything to roam about free as a bird again, instead of wearing himself out with the needs of a larger family."

"You are utterly mistaken, eel," said father reed-warbler. "All I'll admit is..."

"You better watch what you say mate... or else," screamed his mate, taking a poke at him.

"You need to wiggle," said the eel, disappearing.

In the afternoon, the two of them talked about their situation again.

*   *   *

"I hope we can keep going," he said. "The other day, I fought for all I was worth with a flycatcher friend over a little, ridiculous larva. I won, so he'll never forgive me."

"Who knows if it will get any worse than it is," she said. "You know what I do? I think about all the beautiful things that the poets have composed about us. It always helps to keep me in a joyful mood."

"I'd rather feed a few young poets to the youngsters," he said sarcastically.

They were both lost in their deep thoughts, while the youngsters were taking a mid-day nap.

"The world is a strange place," he blurted. "We, free-as-a-lark birds, for whom the entire world is an open book, have so many grievances and cares, and yet, look at the waterlily. It stays in the same place, and for days on end it must stretch itself up through the murky water until it reaches the surface. There it unfurls its white flower and is happy. See how it sways there, only dreaming, without a care in the world. Oh, if only Mother Nature had made us waterlilies."

"Yes, I see your point," said the mother reed-warbler, "and its seeds ripen in its lap, slide down into the water, settle in the mud where the roots grow, and then in the following year, it flowers all around. Oh, how lovely that must be."

"Yes, but remember how the bladderwort made fools of us," he reminded her.

"Oh, that's nonsense," she insisted. "It was that horrible water spider living with it which caused it to become mean. No one can convince me there is anything but peace and happiness in the waterlily's cup."

"Hush now," interrupted her mate. "It's talking with a nearby cute water buttercup."

The two busy-body birds leaned their heads over and eavesdropped.

✳   ✳   ✳

"You spiteful, nasty creature!" said the waterlily. "You've lured two bumble bees from me today, but you've no more nectar in your withered cup than what's on the smallest part of me."

"You can scold me as much as you want," said the water buttercup. "Your fancy florescence won't help you at all. The bumble bee is searching for genuine sources of nectar, and it wouldn't give a second look at a floozie like you. I have more stored nectar in one of my blossoms than you have in every part of you."

"I'm standing here with all of my pollen ripe," said the waterlily. "and I can't give it away. It's a wonder anyone wants to look at a tramp like you, but now, I'll take my revenge. You've annoyed me all the time we've been growing up together; your skinny, disgusting stems climb all over me and would have chocked me if they could. What a piece of trash you are. By fall there isn't a fiber left on you, and it's incredible that you're allowed to stand in the way of the higher ranks in this lake."

"In the fall, my seeds are ripe and sown, you prissy, little waterlily," replied the water buttercup. "And next spring, they'll sprout out and annoy you just like I'm doing now. You can count on it."

"If those humans don't come and clean up the lake beforehand," said the waterlily. "They'll get rid of you but let me stay because I'm so beautiful."

The water buttercup couldn't say anything about that, because it was true.

"Did you hear that?" whispered mother reed-warbler. "She's not so happy after all."

"Hush," replied the reed-warbler, "there's a bumblebee coming."

A loud buzzing filled the air, and a bumblebee flew in, whirring its wings and hovering in the air above the two flowers.

"Please, bumblebee," cried the waterlily, spreading its white petals as best it could. "I have the freshest nectar in the entire lake, and I am offering it to you. Can you come closer, please? My whole cup is full, my lovely pollen awaits you, and I have placed my wide, green leaves out on the water upon which you can rest if you get tired. Look, it's dry right here. Okay?"

"Don't bother yourself with that witch," said the water buttercup. "There is a real old-fashioned nectar supply here with me. I have no use for that silly, outrageous way of advertising yourself with large white petals and all that puffery. Who needs it! I concentrate on my nectar and pollen with just a little yellow flower so you can find me."

"You shouldn't dream of going into that greasy imposter!" cried the waterlily. "All the junk it has will poison your young ones, if it has anything left worth sharing. Two bumblebees were there today, and they appeared annoyed when they flew away."

"Don't believe that annoying waterlily," replied the water buttercup. "It is spouting off from pure envy. The delighted bumblebees were here, and they got an enormous amount of nectar. Waterlilies are yesterday's plant, and no one wants to touch them anymore. I swear, they are utterly corrupt."

"Oh, I haven't got time for this nonsense!" said the bumblebee and flew away.

"What a cheeky fellow," said the waterlily.

"What a lowlife," said the water buttercup.

"That's what you get from keeping awful company," said the waterlily.

"That's what you get for exaggerating," said the water buttercup. sinking "Decent folks move away from the lake because of you."

The two antagonists couldn't find anything else to say, so they floated on the water, trying to look mean at each other.

"Well, listen to that!" said reed-warbler, "but where in the world can we go to find peace and friendship? Where is there poetry?"

"Where can I find a fly?" inquired her mate.

"Accept life as it is," said the clam, "and mix yourself up with as few creatures as possible. That what I do, and I can remain here for a hundred years."

At that moment, a boy standing on the shore tossed a large stone out into the water with all his might. Then he left without giving it so much as a thought. But the sinking stone had struck the clam head on and crushed its shells.

"Look now," gasped the clam. "He smashed both my shells, and there's nothing to do about it. What's done is done. Goodbye world... and thanks for your sympathetic company, reed-warblers."

All its eyes burst, one after the other, along the remaining rim of the shell, and then it died.

"I wonder who's next?" said the reed-warbler as mother crayfish came crawling along and grabbed the dead clam with her claws.

"Now I'll get my leg back and more besides," she said.

The Travels of The Crayfish

"How's it going with my little larva?" inquired the mother reed-warbler.

"Okay, thanks," said the mayfly larva. A roach fish tried to eat me, as did two spring fly larvae who tore into me, and a bigger creature bit me in one leg. Otherwise, I'm fine."

"Aren't you almost finished with your life cycle?"

"Today or tomorrow, probably."

"Watch out then you don't have an accident beforehand," said mother reed-warbler kindly before her mood darkened at the sight of mother crayfish who was crawling around restlessly.

"There isn't much to eat," she said. "If only I was a noble bird who could fly away to seek food elsewhere."

The mother reed-warbler just looked down her beak at the crayfish.

"Okay, I know you are angry with me, so I hesitate to say a word to you," said the crayfish after a deep sigh. Her look was so sad, mother reed-warbler softened her attitude a little.

"True, I have been furious with you," she replied, "but I have since experienced many terrible things, so our differences have slipped from my mind. I made the acquaintance of a water spider that ate her mother."

"Good gracious!" said the crayfish. "That must really make any mother angry."

"It should. She also ate her mate."

"I won't argue that's right," said crayfish, "but it's more excusable, because males are nothing but monsters. Yes, I make an exception for your mate."

"You have loose morals, too, mother crayfish," said reed-warbler. "Tell me... did you really eat your own newborns?"

"Unfortunately, I ate seven of them," said the crayfish with an unhappy expression on her face. "But, truly, it was only from pure love. They were so wonderful, but I patted them too hard with my claws. Then it was better that I ate them than to leave them for some stranger."

"Such a horrible thing to hear," said mother reed-warbler.

"Yes, it is so sad," said the crayfish. "But, forgive me, they're gone now, the poor little things. But their one hundred and ninety-three brothers and sisters are battling it out in the cruel, wide world. Who knows how many are still living, and how they are surviving?"

"Yes, the world is an unforgiving place," said reed-warbler.

"Will you tell me something, please? As a mother, don't you think someone like me could leave the lake?" asked crayfish.

"We're leaving in the fall," replied reed-warbler. "For Italy. But you don't have any wings, crayfish, so I don't understand how you'll get away."

"That just it. If you have wings, you can soon be on your way. But perhaps they would be an inconvenience in the water. And there are those without wings can still travel. What do you say about the eel, for example?"

"Oh yes, the eel," said the reed-warbler. "It can wiggle, but you can't do that."

"Indeed not," replied the crayfish, her eyes filled with sadness. "I can't do that because of my stiff outer shell, but I'm glad of that. If I had the ability, I would have ventured away from here a long time ago."

"So, what are you going to do?"

The crayfish crawled right under the reeds where the nest was hanging and asked softly: "What do you think about the clam?"

"The clam?"

"Yes, the clam. I'm always sitting here in the muck hearing so many different conversations. What about the story the clam told you and your mate the other day... do you think it's believable?"

"Yes, I do," responded mother reed-warbler.

"Well, I don't think much of that clam creature," said crayfish. "Such a mollusk; she insulted me, so I ate her, but I don't like to talk down about what I eat. It's possible another one will come along, and it'll meet up with the same fate."

"But you don't have a shell to squeeze with, crayfish... right?"

"No, but I have my claws," replied the crayfish, "and believe me, they can also hold on tight."

With that, she crawled off again, and when father reed-warbler had returned from searching for food, his mate told him about the crayfish plans. They both giggled at this but hadn't realized how stubborn the crayfish was. Later that morning, done with crawling around the bottom, the crayfish swam up to the surface of the lake in order to see if there was any possible prey. At noon time, a little roach fish came swimming by.

"Be careful, larva," cried mother reed-warbler.

"I'm hiding under a leaf, and everything is just fine," replied the mayfly larva.

"There's the roach fish," muttered the crayfish treading water, and scouting to all sides with her long eyes. "Now all I need is a seagull."

"What are you up to, you disgusting crayfish?" said the roach fish flipping its tail.

"Oh, you silly fish, I'm not about to do anything to you," she replied. "Isn't the lake for everybody. Can't I take a breath of fresh air outside my own house?"

The eel stuck her head up from the deep. "That's right, crayfish, hang in there," she said. "You've got to wiggle."

The reed-warblers laughed at that but kept peeking down, wondering what would happen next. Their youngsters, growing bigger every day, imitated their parents. The water spider also came running to watch, and the mayfly larva was about to crack its pupa case out of curiosity. The bladderwort forgot to hunt for prey, and the waterlily and the water buttercup stopped quarreling as they were all waiting to see what the crayfish and roach fish were up to. They had all sensed something was about to happen, but none of them said anything so as not to chase the roach fish away who was the only one who didn't suspect the slightest. Only the reeds whispered quietly to each other. But they do that all the time, so no one pays any attention to them.

As this was happening, a seagull attacked the roach fish.

There was a gigantic splash in the water—no one could really see what was happening—but then the roach fish was gone, and immediately the reed-warblers screamed:

"Look, look... there's the seagull with the roach fish trapped in its beak... and the crayfish is hanging on to one of the seagull legs with its back claw!"

The waterlily, the water buttercup, and the rushes cried out in surprise, and word travelled so fast across the lake that soon there wasn't even a gnat larva who didn't know what strange events had occurred.

"So, it was a successful plan," said the mother reed-warbler to her mate.

They chatted for a long time about how it all might end, but no one could really figure it out, nor did anyone in the whole lake ever learn more about it.

Only the woman who lived by the lake knew what happened. When the gull was above the chimney of her little cottage, the gull gave such a leg kick that the crayfish fell away, right through the chimney and into a pot of her boiling water.

"Yikes!" said the crayfish. "That not where I intended to go!" So embarrassed, the former mother crayfish blushed a deep red over her whole body and died immediately.

Meanwhile, the woman picked up her kettle of boiling water and was about to pour it into a bag full of coffee grounds when she stared with amazement at the large, delightful crayfish floating dead in front of her.

"Oh well!" she said. "Thanks so much." Then she ate the crayfish.

* * *

That same evening, the mayfly larva broke out of her pupa case and rose in flight into the air on tiny, thin, transparent wings with three long threads on her abdomen for keeping balance.

"Oh, how lovely it is here," she said. "Life is so delightful. I can tolerate those many days as a poor larva if only for the chance to have one hour of life to see this magnificent sight."

"Oh, are you there?" said mother reed-warbler. "You look just fine."

"Thank you," said the mayfly. "Now I'm going to fly around and lay my eggs. Then I'll return, settle down in the reeds and die, after which you can eat me. Many thanks to you for sparing my life, and for warning me when I was in danger. If you hadn't done that, I never would have gotten to see all this loveliness."

"I hope you won't stuff yourself somewhere, get lost, and forget your promise," said reed-warbler.

"No chance of that," replied the mayfly. "I have eaten what there is to eat; I don't even have a mouth part. I'm just going to enjoy myself for a couple of hours in this lovely nature and then go lay my eggs. That's my fate, and I'm not complaining at all."

"Life isn't so splendid as you think," said reed-warbler. "If I was your true friend, I'd have spared you from seeing all your illusions shattered."

"But how can you say that life is not wonderful?" said the mayfly. "Look here..."

"I'll be your real friend," interrupted the mother reed-warbler, "so you'll be saved from disappointment. I'm going to eat you now."

So, she grabbed the mayfly and ate her.

*   *   *

"Good evening," said the eel. "Are you looking out at nature? I saw that you just dispatched... hmm, the mayfly. Now, that's nice. By the way, how did she taste?"

"You're a horrible, vile fellow," said mother reed-warbler. "I showed her pity."

"It makes me happy that you are so practiced now in reed-warbler skills," replied the eel, with a smirk on his face.

The Beginning of the End

It was late summer. The beech foliage was streaked in yellow, and the lake was overgrown with plants almost out to the middle. All the tadpoles had grown into frogs, and all the other youngsters had grown up too, demanding more food. The waterlily and the water buttercup had stopped annoying each other, because there was nothing left to quarrel about. They had both lost their petals and stood with full seedcases.

The reed-warblers' youngsters had grown so large they were beginning to venture from the nest and flit around the reeds. But they still lacked self-confidence, preferring to hang around their parents, and they never ventured further away so they could easily return to the nest. Every evening they crouched down, argued over positions in the nest, and pecked and kicked each other while their exhausted parents sat on the edge of the nest telling them to be quiet.

"Oh, bring me that fly over there," said one of them to its mother.

"I can't catch that horrible gnat," said another.

"The dragonfly flew away from me," sobbed the third.

"I'm afraid to take the daddy-longlegs," said the fourth.

But the fifth youngster didn't say anything because he was a little weakling who was always gloomy.

"That one will never develop into a fine reed-warbler," said the father.

And when they exercised by flying around, hopping, and climbing in the reeds, or if they were tested for their songs, the fifth one always stood behind from the others.

"We'll never get him all way to Italy," said the reed-warbler, while his mate merely sighed.

Down in the water, the duck was splashing about with the now grown-up ducklings.

"Things are coming to an end," she said. "I notice it with everything, and I have a funny feeling in my bones."

"What nasty thing could happen to you?" asked the reed-warbler. "Since you don't migrate, you don't have to be looking around, like us."

"You never know," said the duck. "I'm wary."

So, she paddled on a bit, quacking after the ducklings in her old, anxious voice and looking very troubled.

One day an event took place that was a cause for uproar around the whole lake. The pike was suddenly pulled out of the water.

Mother reed-warbler saw it herself. It was hanging by a thin string, thrashing around terribly, jumping into the air in big arcs, and finally falling down onto the grass. At the end of the string there was a stick, and at the other end of the stick there was a boy who was flushed with excitement over the large fish he had caught with his home-made fishing tackle.

"Good for him, that bandit," said the perch.

"Let's have a party! That pike is gone," croaked the frogs, and all the small roach fish and carps jumped for joy.

"He didn't have many friends," said reed-warbler.

"He didn't have any," said the perch. "He was the worst thief in the lake."

"He never did anything to me," said the waterlily. "He was a smart, distinguished fish who shone over all of you. It was always a true pleasure for me when he swished his body among my stems."

"I've seen so many fish swishing into him," said the eel. "But they didn't think it was so much fun. He never did anything I wouldn't have done if I had been in his place. But now he's gone, and I suppose I'm now the largest one in the lake."

The eel stretched to his whole length.

"You've gotten big and fat," said reed-warbler.

"It's been a good year," replied the eel. "But soon I'll be wiggling out to the ocean again, and that will run the fat off me."

The same evening a man was standing at the edge of the lake, a bit away from the area where the reed-warblers were living. He had high boots on and was sharpening his scythe until it could cut the very air.

"What's going to happen now?" said reed-warbler.

"Quack, quack, look out!" screamed the terrified duck, who knew what was happening, but the man spit into his palms and taking hold of the scythe, he walked out into the water and began to mow down a section of the reeds starting at the shore and

moving out as far as it grew. The reeds fell with subdued sighs into the water, and when he was finished, he stood back on the bank surveying his work.

"That makes a good clearing for a hunting blind," he said. "Tomorrow, we'll go for ducks."

Then he continued on with his scythe and made another clearing, so he was happy, but he did terrible harm to the lake. He destroyed the water spider's web and crushed the spider. He broke off the bladderwort by trampling on its roots with his heavy rubber boots. In the fallen reeds, the reed-warblers nest had been overturned, and the distraught birds flew out, screaming around the nest.

"Youngsters!" shouted the parents.

Four of them had flapped their way to the shore and sat there looking deeply bewildered, but the fifth one was half buried out in the remaining reeds and couldn't get in any closer. The two parents helped him with difficulty to join his waiting siblings.

"Goodness," said mother reed-warbler anxiously. "What are we going to do now?"

"It could be worse," replied her mate. "Suppose that happened a month ago. Now the youngsters can take care of themselves except for the decrepit over there."

"How did we get into this terrible situation?" she demanded of her mate. "It was a dumb thing for you to drag me up here. I think I'd rather have stayed in Italy and never gotten to know you and start a family."

"Just answer me one thing," he replied. "Didn't you long to come up here as much as I did? We're born here; this is our home, and this is where we must build our nest. It's in our nature, something we ought not to try and change. We've had a memorable time here with each other, mostly good, only sometimes not. So, let's not quarrel about the bygone days but get the youngsters prepared for the trip and be on our way."

His mate calmed down, and they sat out and talked into the night about it. The four healthy youngsters ran around on the grass eating gnats and thinking the whole thing was a lot of fun, because the young ones usually don't understand these complicated discussions. Only the fifth youngster was looking sad with his head hanging down.

"What are we going to do with the weakling," said mother reed-warbler feeding it a bite. "We'll never get it to Italy with us."

*   *   *

Quite early the next morning, there was an enormous scene at the lake. Men were yelling, and dogs were barking. A rowboat was in the lake, moving with difficulty through all the duckweed, and the woman who ate the crayfish was standing outside her cottage, curtsying to the patrons and serving beer.

"What in heaven's name is happening?" said the father reed-warbler.

"It's the end of the world," said the duck. "Quack! quack! quack!"

"Get to the bottom! Go!" said the eel. "You need to wiggle."

Terrified, the reed-warbler family initially huddled together in the grass, but the reed-warblers became so curious that they couldn't contain themselves. The parent reed-warblers ordered the youngsters to be very quiet regardless of what was happening and positioned themselves a little away from each other on the tops of the remaining reeds by the side of the clearing.

Suddenly, the loud "Bang! Bang! Bang!" of gunfire from rifles resounded over the lake.

There were many ducks quacking, and many small frightened birds flew from their hiding places. Large, ferocious dogs with their tongues hanging out of their mouths were swimming about; others were barking. The leaves of the waterlilies were under the water, while the water buttercups simply disappeared, and weren't seen again.

"Bang! Bang! Bang!"

"There lies our duck," said mother reed-warbler, trembling.

The duck they'd often chatted with lay motionless, belly up on the water, waiting only for the dog to come and get her.

"Bang! Bang!"

"I'm leaving; I can't stand it," said mother reed-warbler. "Let's return to the youngsters."

She didn't get an answer, and when she looked around, her mate was gone.

She looked around in the reed stand where he had been sitting, and then down in the water. She then gave a piercing scream.

"Oh, I'm a poor, deserted widow. What am I going to do? What is left for me?"

He was lying in the water, hit by some passing shot, stone dead and gone for good.

"Your father is dead!" she yelled to her youngsters.

The four of them looked terrified at each other when she arrived with the news, but the fifth reacted without concern as it usually did to any event.

Out on the lake, a fierce commotion was in progress. The six reed-warblers sat in a row on the shore and didn't have an inkling about what to do, but at last it quieted down again.

The dust from the gunpowder blew away, and the water became still. The hunters were sitting in the woods having lunch, and the woman of the lake was counting the money she had earned from the beer.

"That was a terrible episode," said the waterlily.

"My mate is dead," said mother reed-warbler, singing a touching lament.

"I'm so sorry for you," said the eel coming out of the muck. "But won't you now give me some credit, and tell me I was right? Think how much sorrow and inconvenience you save by being free of that family nonsense. I don't know my mate and I have never even seen her, as I've already told you. I wouldn't shed one tear if someone told me that she was dead."

"You ugly, heartless creature!" said the mourning mother reed-warbler. "How can you speak like that to a widow with five dependent ones, including one that is also disabled?"

"You females!" said the eel and disappeared.

✳   ✳   ✳

In the evening mother reed-warbler was sitting, thinking things over.

"We need to leave," she said to her young ones. "This very night. There's nothing else for us to do here. We'll fly, we'll hop, we'll do the best we can, and if we're careful and you behave yourselves, everything will turn out alright."

I can't go along with you," said the disabled youngster.

She looked for a moment at the poor thing that she had neglected. Then she shook her wings and made a final decision.

"No, you can't follow along with us," she said, "and the rest of us cannot remain here and perish for your sake. If I leave you behind, you'll be eaten by a fox or a cat or those horrible ants. It would be a shame if you suffered, poor little thing. So, I'd rather end your life myself right now."

She charged at the youngster, pecking it in the head until it was dead.

Then she said to the others: "We must leave now, all together."

"You mustn't leave until I've said goodbye to you," interrupted the eel. "I've decided you're actually a decent mother who understands how to adapt to circumstances. You were full of bitterness toward the rotten thieves in the lake, but still, you ate innocent flies yourself from morning to night. You say you love poetry, but you ate the poor mayfly even though you gave her your word that she could live an hour of her life like nature intended. You were furious at the water spider who ate her mother, and at crayfish who consumed her own offspring, and now blatantly, willfully, you pecked your own disabled young one to death so that you could leave for Italy."

"Oh, thank goodness I'll never see you again, you rotten, disgusting creature!" said reed-warbler. "For your information, I sacrificed my child out of pity for it."

"And the water spider ate her mother to prevent starving to death, and the crayfish from love of hers," said the eel. "It was just clever of me to let my own offspring shift for themselves."

"Young ones," pronounced reed-warbler. "Can you believe it? The eel was designed to live in this horrible lake, he says."

They then all flew away together.

"I don't think I'll stay here anyway," said the eel. "I'm longing for the sea."

Looking around carefully, he crawled up onto the grass, and wiggled himself skillfully over to the closest ditch. "Bye, bye, lake," he said.

The End

November arrived as usual. The trees stood with bare branches; the dropped leaves were rustling on the ground or floating on the lake. All the reeds had been cut down. The leaves of the water-lilies, the stems, everything was withering away, but down at the bottom, it was time for the waterlily's winter rest and to dream of its new springtime, white flowery display.

Also, in the lake at the deepest bottom, all the frogs were lying in the muck so that only their noses were sticking up. It looked like the lake bottom was paved with only frog noses, looking like cobblestones in the street. Lakeside, the trees were leafless like the woods up on land. Hidden among stalks and dried leaves, under stones and in the muck, all the animals were sleeping, or their eggs were waiting for spring to come so they could crack and break open.

All the birds had flown away except the chaffinch and a couple others that hopped about, surviving as best they could. All the flies were gone, including the dragonflies, the water spiders, the ants, and the butterflies. Only a few sulky, hungry fish remained in the lake.

And storms shook the trees, so they groaned and whipped up the lake, making high waves with foam tops.

"It's really awful here in the winter," said the woman of the lake who was filling in the cracks around her windows with moss.

"Do you hear?" she said to herself. "Listen to the howl in the chimney, a creaking and a crashing in the woods, a humming and a buzzing on the lake. If only we had our wonderful summer back? What a happy and peaceful time it is then to live at the lake."

* * *

On a path around the lake, however, a guide was walking with seven ladies.

He had a warm jacket on with the collar up around his ears, and the ladies were all wrapped up too, so that you could only see the tip of their noses. It was very cold.

"My dear ladies," said the guide. "When you now look at this depressing, unwelcoming, not very appealing lake, you can't imagine how wonderful it is in the summertime. Just now, the uncaring elements are all out in force, wave smacks against wave, it is stormy, and the trees look pitiful in their nakedness. It is truly a picture of sorrow, stress, and cruelty."

"But take a walk out here on a summer day, my ladies, and you'll have another view. Then, reeds grow beautifully along the shore, waterlilies and water buttercups suspend side by side on the surface of the lake, nodding and smiling at each other with their flowery cups. The gnats are dancing in the air; frogs are croaking, and happy birds are singing. Deep in the water, there are lovely fish swimming around playing cheerfully with their fins outstretched. The clams are dreaming in the depths about making lovely pearls, the crayfish are crawling slowly around enjoying life, and being happy with each other."

"Dear ladies, you haven't any idea what a feeling of peace and contentment arises from this lake. It's a feeling of unity in nature, the whole of a marvelous, in-tune, perfectly coordinated nature, whose spectacle consoles us poor people who fight and bicker from morning to night, and then envy, slander, and persecute each other.

Dear ladies, don't forget to walk out here when summer comes. It strengthens you, helps you to take on your own fierce, inner battles, to see the happiness in which nature's lower creatures live—yes, those lacking the great gift of self-consciousness like us, but who have truly a purer, deeper joy, living in peace with one another."

The guide continued speaking like this, and the seven ladies listened respectfully to him. And none of them interrupted.

What did they know? What did the guide really know?

The Tadpoles

It was now late in March. The ice had long since disappeared from all the lakes, and the snow had melted leaving so much water running into the ditches, it overflowed the banks. Only deep under the bushes were suggestions of something lively lying on the ground. But it was so tiny and black that no one paid the least attention to it.

After being covered throughout the winter, the grass felt ashamed of being so yellow and inquired down into the ground if the new grass wouldn't be ready soon to spring out again for the new year. The violets carefully opened up their blue eyes, and the buds on the trees were working day and night to look their best for the springtime.

Each day, all the plants and trees and flowers got bigger and brighter and greener, and on one lovely spring day, the gooseberry bush finally lost its patience and sprang out. The bush stood there, its tiny new leaves quivering, unable to resist the temptation to take in the new warmth. As it did so, the sun peeped down between the drifting clouds and called out over the earth:

"I'm coming now! I'm coming now! Just work hard, and everything will turn out great for you!"

However, sitting on the edge of the ditch deep in the woods, the starling was considering she felt lonely, and the nights were still cold. When looking for food, there were only the barest necessities, but the starling would rather arrive from her winter habitat a month too early than one day too late.

She told herself life wasn't so bad, and things would get better, so after she cleaned and groomed her feathers, she lifted her bill into the air and whistled a tune to keep her good mood going. When she tired of her music, she laid her black head to one side, closed her eyes, and listened to the running water in the ditch which rippled and sang its own tune.

"Sing some more please, ditch!" she begged. "Sing about the summer when you'll be dry and silent, and then we'll take over making music because then the days will be full of sunshine, the meadows are full of worms, and I will have a nest full of wonderful young ones."

"Oh, yes," said a gruff frog voice nearby. "But for those who provide for the newly born, nature also brings unhappiness."

The starlings looked around and caught sight of a large, green frog which stared at her with sad eyes.

"Oh, it's you, frog, happy springtime!" chirped the starling, seeming to forget that only recently she'd felt grumpy. "Why are you so sad? Such talk! Naturally, it takes a lot of work to have a nest full of young ones. They are hungry, screaming to eat something, and I've done a good day's work just stuffing food down their throats before I can eat myself and rest. But it's also wonderful to sit in the nest with them in the evening and sing. Don't you feel the same way?"

"Croak!" replied the frog testily.

The starling made believe she hadn't heard the frog, and calmly continued: "And it's even lovelier to see the newborns grow up and get eyes and wings, and a tail too. Then I can teach them to fly and catch worms."

"Croak, croak, croak!" muttered the frog and hopped off with three gigantic leaps.

"I'm not sure what you meant with your croaking?" said the starling, "but it sounds rude."

Before the starling even finished, the frog sprang headfirst into the ditch with a hefty splash and then put her forelegs up against her chest and made an enormous push-off with her back legs. She swam back and forth three or four times, then hopped out of the water again, sat down at her old place next to the starling and just gazed out into the air with a melancholy look.

The starling sang a little, gentle melody, and then said:

"Did my singing help, frog? You seem bothered by something, but you shouldn't take life so seriously. Tell me, what's the problem? It helps sometimes to unburden the heart, and I'm quite bored."

"You wouldn't understand even if I told you," said the frog. "What does an elegant bird like you know about my problems? You have your own neat, cozy nest, and can raise your youngsters up to be good-natured birds. Others don't have it so great. I don't have a nest at all, and I have to neglect my babies."

"You don't have a nest?" inquired the amazed starling. "Where do you lay your eggs?"

"Down there," answered the frog, pointing toward the ditch below with her head. "I've just been checking up on them."

"In the water?"

"Yes, of course!" said the frog. "Nothing strange about that. My eggs don't have a hard shell around them like yours, and if I laid them here on the land, they would just dry out immediately and die."

"Can your babies then swim right away?" asked the starling.

"Yes, they can, thank goodness," answered the frog. "Our family has it in their blood. But actually, they are so naughty, and it will be the death of me."

"What are they doing?" asked the starling.

"Come look for yourself!" said the frog.

She hopped along to the edge of the ditch, and the starling walked behind because she was curious and didn't want to miss a thing at this time of the year. When they came to a place where the ditch widened out into a small, undisturbed pool, the frog stopped.

The frog looked pitifully up at the starling but said nothing.

The water was full of tiny animals that were swimming back and forth, up and down, and nipping at the aquatic plants. They had no legs, but enormously fat tummies, and long thin, transparent tails. They resembled little balls attached to a small pointy stick, and on each side of their heads, they had a bushy appearing knob, which they waved in the water.

"Well, well!" said the starling and licked her chops. "They look so delicious, and... wouldn't they taste good? They are fish, yes?"

"I don't know what they are," the frog replied, "but they have come out of my eggs, and I don't believe there has ever been fish in our family. I've never been a mother before, and I never knew my parents, so no one told me anything."

"Wait a second," said the starling thoughtfully. "I heard about this once, but I unfortunately don't remember it that well anymore. The only thing I know is that you were probably once like they are, and so they will eventually develop into proper frogs like you. You'll probably get some pleasure out of them, but not until they have learned how to get along in this world."

"Sure, but they must get legs before they can be adults," replied the frog. "Tails? Look at those tails! Has anyone seen a frog with a tail? And what a tummy! You can even see all their guts right through the skin. And what a funny dingle-dangle hanging at their necks... oh, where are their legs?"

The starling put out a wing trying to comfort the frog, but she just kept talking.

"See how they dart around in the water eating junk when the most luscious insects are swimming by right by in front of their noses. Oh, what have I done? My babies are such freaks!"

The frog began to weep bitterly, and the starling figured she ought to leave because she didn't like sad events and she had only just gotten herself into a good mood. But all at once, with another big jump, the frog was back in the ditch, swimming over to a stone which jutted out from the surface of the water, and crawled up onto it.

"There's that whacky, old one!" yelled the small tadpoles. "Now we'll have some fun!"

They all laughed at once, so their fat tummies shook, and their throats quivered with delight as they swam around the rock. Then, in full voice, they sang:

Look at silly old frog
Sitting on a stone.

Thinks she's some kind of queen
Sitting on her throne.

Who would want to be like her?
Hopping here and there,

We'd rather swim around, it's fun
About frogs we don't care.

Twice they sang their naughty verse, and tears ran down the cheeks of the frog.

"Now you can see for yourself," the frog blubbered to the starling. "That's the way they talk to their own mother."

"Well," answered the starling thoughtfully, "it isn't very nice to hear."

The little tadpoles now swam away from the stone, giggling as they did so. When the frog had dried her eyes and recovered some, she saw that they had all left except for one still in the water just under the stone wiggling her tail.

"Shame on you!" shouted the frog. "Look at her, still there, making a fool of her old mother. Some grateful youngster, you are!"

"I'm not an ordinary 'youngster', as you say," she replied. "I'm a tadpole."

"Well, just wait until I get done with you... you show-off!" replied the frog. "You don't even deserve the frog name! What kind of freak are you?"

The tadpole swam back and forth a couple of times and nipped at some plants. Then she returned under the stone and said:

"You're always howling and reprimanding us; for you, nothing in the world is right. I don't understand why you are making such a fuss, mother frog. You probably don't remember, but you were once a youngster yourself?"

"Don't I?" replied the frog, annoyed. "In my youth, we were far more respectful and proper, you spoiled brat! When I was young, I didn't go around in the water with such nonsense in my head. Shame on you all."

"That's news to me," said the tadpole, flicking her bushy prominent head with pleasure. "Aren't they pretty? By the way, they are my gills. If I didn't have them, I couldn't breathe under water."

The mother frog shook with anger.

"So, now you have gills... you upstart!" she said. "And you have a lovely long tail to wag. But can't you equip yourself with ordinary legs?"

"What would I do with them?" asked the tadpole nonchalantly. "Maybe you need them to hop around with, up on the ground where you hang out, but I need to swim, which is what my tail is for. That's in fashion now for tadpoles. We don't mess with all that old-fashioned, hoppity-hoppity slow stuff. Styles change and we have to follow the times."

"Good gracious," said the frog. She shook her head, folded her forelegs over her chest and looked up to the sky in desperation.

"It's impossible to talk sense with a silly creature like you," interjected the tadpole. "You don't understand anything; your time is over. Remember, you brought me into this world, and so now you have to take me as I am."

Whereupon, she swam away, and the frog moved back to the edge of the ditch where she sat down next to the starling. She didn't know how to console the frog, so she whistled a happy tune; the frog still looked forlorn.

"Spring is coming, and everything will be fine again, you'll see. Where were you this winter?" asked the starling, thinking to change the subject.

"I've been sitting in a hole down at the bottom of the mill pond," the frog replied.

"Well, that could get you depressed," said the starling. "You should take a trip. It gets you going again and puts you in a good mood."

"What are you driving at?" responded the frog. "With my figure, I'm designed to take it easy. Even with just a hop across the field, I can feel it in my hind legs."

The starling decided she was wasting her time and flew away without another word. As the frog gazed up at the starling, wondering what it was like to fly, a fat fly buzzed past. The frog snapped it with her tongue, thinking that a snack might help. The minute she swallowed the insect, she fell into her melancholy mood again.

* * *

A few days later, the starling was busy stuffing and sealing up her nest in the birdhouse sitting in the elm tree outside the forest ranger's house. She had found her handsome mate and could feel that it would soon be time to lay her eggs; she felt strangely bothered by this, and once in a while, she even cried. Thinking of the poor frog that she hadn't seen for a long time, she flew to the edge of the ditch once more and called out to her. The frog was still on the edge of the ditch.

"I'm here... I'm here, starling," announced the frog sitting close by.

"What's this," replied the starling. "Still sitting here? How are the little ones? I will be a mother soon myself, so I was thinking about you."

"That's sweet of you to look in on a poor mother," answered the frog. "Actually, things are looking a little brighter for me, I think."

"How so?" inquired the starling, glad she was not going to be faced with a grumpy frog again.

The frog beckoned to the starling, and she hopped right close to the water.

"See for yourself?" the mother frog said.

The starling peeked down into the ditch full of tadpoles. They were swimming around in a lively way, just like the last time but not only had they grown much larger, and some of them had the cutest little frog hind legs you would ever want to see; a couple of the biggest ones even had small forelegs.

"It's something, don't you think?" said the mother frog, now seeming to care for her little ones. "They're beginning to behave themselves better. They still have those nasty tails and that nuisance blob hanging around their heads, but I can now see that there is some purpose to them. So, I hold my tongue and I don't scold them anymore. I think it's best to let nature take its course, even though they can also be irritating. The other day when I was praising one of them because she was showing some sense, she just grinned at me and said she could never imagine becoming an old nag like me. Oh dear, these youngsters, these juveniles! I hope you have better luck with yours.

"Thanks," responded the starling, "but now I am flying home to start my family."

*　　*　　*

For many days, the starling sat upon her eggs in the birdhouse in the elm tree and never thought about the frog. But as she noticed that the eggs were on the verge of opening so the young ones could come out soon, she asked her mate, while he had the time, to fly out to the ditch and bring greetings to the frog from her.

"Mother frog has also given birth," she said. "The poor thing has had such a hard time with her newborns. We need to show her a little sympathy."

She told her mate everything she had seen and heard at the ditch, and he flew down to see what was happening.

But no matter how hard he peeked into the water, he couldn't see any tadpoles. The ditch was already half dried out but down in the mud, an old, fat toad was crawling around.

Then the starling heard an enormous noise coming from the meadow across on the other side of the ditch. "Croak! Croak! Croak!" There were a bunch of frogs jabbering at each other to see which one could croak the loudest. The mother frog was sitting in the middle of a circle in the grass surrounded by her newly, fully formed young ones who were now leaping around and falling over each other.

All of them now had their legs, and not one of them had the bump from the gill mass on their heads. Close up, they appeared as small, attractive brown frogs whose moist skin glistened in the sunshine, and who said "croak!" so loudly that it startled you. But they all had a little piece of tail still left from their youth.

"Okay, you upstarts!" said mother frog. "Keep your wits about you. I'm so happy for you, really overjoyed. Soon, you'll lose that disgusting little piece of tail, and then everything will be just fine."

Now there were some young frogs who were sitting in such a way that you couldn't see their tails. They tilted their heads to one side and now looked lovingly at the older frog.

"We don't have tails at all anymore! We are real frogs now, dear mother, and we never meant to upset you with our childish, tadpole nonsense chatter."

But there were others who showed off their tails, swishing them to the front as much as they could, and laughing at their mother just like they did when they were still tadpoles.

"Silly old frog!" they yelled. "We' re just like we have always been; can't you see our tails? Don't fool yourself into believing that we have become sensible, or 'keeping our wits' as you call it. That, we'll never be. We will always be free, jolly tadpoles."

The mother frog scolded, and when that didn't work, begged them to simmer down, but the youngsters shouted and screamed, and it was a terrible scene. The starling shook his black head and flew home to tell his mate what he had seen.

"They are a rowdy family," he reported to his mate.

"They are an unhappy family," added mother starling. "As soon as I can, I'll take a walk with the nestlings. It will be good for them to see a bit of the world, to better appreciate their own good home."

*　　*　　*

When the young ones had opened their eyes, put on some feathers, and learned to fly a little, their mother took them for a walk into the meadow in order that they might say hello to mother frog. They walked a long way, searching and calling to her, and finally they found her under a large field stone.

"Well," said the starling. "Now I have raised my family, as you can see. How are you doing? Where are the youngsters?"

"They left a long time ago," said the frog. "They spread over the whole meadow now and are taking care of themselves."

"That's nice," said the starling. "And how do you think they are getting along?"

"Oh, wonderful!" answered the frog. "They are the most delightful frogs you can imagine. They leap around, and they say 'Croak'! I couldn't wish for nicer youngsters."

"All is well that ends well," said the starling.

"That's true," replied the frog. "You're right. But the beginning was definitely rough. And can you imagine this: One day, when they were all grown up, when their tails and tadpole features were all gone, I chatted with them about those early days. They stared at me with eyes that said they didn't remember a thing, and they laughed at me, hardly letting me even talk about it. Finally, one of them said that it was probably because I had provided them with a messy upbringing. When she had her newborns, she would teach them how to behave if they began to act naughty... like little monkeys."

"I ask you: What do you say to all this, considering how I lectured them, struggled, and put myself out for them?"

"Well... youngsters are not always grateful," said the starling.

"Indeed," replied the frog. "They still had to obey me, and that's the most important thing. In the winter, hibernating in our holes at the bottom of the millpond, no one will see how they lived it up in their youth... and made fun of their own mother."

The Dragonfly
and the Waterlily

A medium size stream flowed gently between green bushes and trees, while along the water's edge, tall and erect rushes whispered with the wind. Out on the water, tethered to the stream's bottom by its green stems, a waterlily was afloat, proudly showing off its yellow-white flower and broad green leaves.

Occasionally, strong winds whipped up the water and it even tore at the rushes. When this happened, the waterlily's flower was sometimes submerged under the waves, while its green leaves were lifted up into the air, standing on edge. The thick green stems supporting the waterlily from the bottom had a hard time of it and struggled to hang on. However, it never moved, always staying in the same place and on the surface, and once the wind had gone, it retained its calm and serene appearance.

On the stem of a waterlily, a larva was crawling up and down. "Golly, being a waterlily must be so boring," the larva said, looking up at the waterlily's flower. "Stuck in one place all the time."

"You talk like you know something about me," replied the waterlily haughtily. "Feeling beautiful is just the loveliest thing in this world."

"Well, I'm puzzled," said the larva. "I'd like to immediately tear myself loose and zoom around in the air just like the big, wonderful dragonfly does."

"Well... you might think that would be a nice thing to do!" the waterlily said sarcastically. "I'd rather just lie quietly, while I soak up the warm sunshine, and occasionally be rocked by the gentle waves. That's the ticket!"

The larva remained silent for a moment, thinking about what the waterlily said.

"I'd rather be something more interesting than that, like a dragonfly with large stiff wings flying along the stream, kissing your lovely white flower, resting a second on your broad leaves, and flying away when it suits me."

"That's ambitious of you, but also dumb," replied the waterlily. "You know what you have, but not what is to come. Let me ask you: How will you manage to be a dragonfly? It doesn't seem like you were born for that. You'll at least have to grow up and be a little prettier; you're very gray and ugly now."

"Yeah, that's too bad for me," said the larva downheartedly. "I'm not sure what the future holds for me, but I hope something will happen. So, for now, I'll just crawl around down here, eating all the vermin that I can find."

"Oh, so you think just by eating, you'll become something greater?" asked the waterlily, laughing. "That's a funny way to imagine what it takes. You'll just become bigger, but still gray and ugly."

"You may well think that, but it's the only way for me," blurted the larva excitedly. "I eat all day long getting fat, and one day I expect that fat will become gold-tinted wings and everything else that will transform me into a real dragonfly."

The waterlily shook its wise white flower.

"Forget your foolish ideas and be happy with the fate you have. You can mess around in peace and quiet down here amongst my leaves and crawl up and down on my stems to your heart's content. You're living very well, with no sorrows and problems, so what more could you possibly want? How do you know life would be better as a dragonfly?"

"You're of a lower order," responded the larva, "with no sense for us higher creatures. I'm going to be a dragonfly and be very happy!"

Then the larva crawled down to the bottom of the waterlily's surface stem to catch prey among its leaves and get even fatter.

But the waterlily remained quietly in place, thinking things over.

"I don't understand animals," it said to itself. "They're busy from morning till night chasing and eating their own kind, and never at peace. We flowers, we're much smarter. Quietly and modestly, we grow up next to each other, soaking up the sunshine, drinking the rainwater, and taking everything as it comes. And I'm the happiest of the bunch. I can float contentedly on the water, while the other land-based flowers are suffering from drought. The fate of us water flowers is the best, but those dumb animals can't understand that."

At sunset, the larva sat quietly on the waterlily's stem with its legs tucked underneath its body. It had eaten its full of vermin and was so fat now that it felt like it was ready to burst. Still, it wasn't pleased about what the waterlily had said, causing it to lie awake the whole night feeling increasingly upset. So much fearful speculation; it wasn't used to that. It also felt miserable with discomfort in its stomach and back, as though they were on the verge of exploding, and then it would quickly die.

As the dawn arrived, it had lost its patience.

"What's going on?" it cried in despair. "I am hurting so badly and can't figure it out. Maybe the waterlily is right, and I'll be nothing but a poor fat larva. Oh, but that is so terribly hard to imagine. I want so much to be a dragonfly, flitting around in the sunshine."

Then suddenly, "Ow... My back! My back! I think I'm about to die."

The larva had the feeling its back was splitting in two, causing it to scream loudly from the pain. At the same time, there was a shivering movement through the rushes at the edges of the stream.

"That's the morning breeze," thought the larva. "I hope I won't die before I see the sunshine again."

So, with great difficulty, it crawled up on one of the waterlily's leaves, stretched its legs fully out, and prepared to die. But when the sun came up in the east, red and round, a hole in the middle of its back appeared. It was a creepy feeling, like something that was narrowly constrained on its back.

"Ow! That hurts like the devil," screamed the larva.

Not knowing what else to do, the larva closed its eyes, but the tightening and pulling kept on inside its body until... suddenly, it opened its eyes again and saw it was now a new and very different creature. And when it looked around properly, it realized it was floating in the air with stiff, shiny wings like a lovely dragonfly!

Down on the waterlily's leaf were the remains of the ugly, gray larval skin.

"Hurray," shouted the new dragonfly. "My wonderful wish has come true!"

Quickly, it flew away for all it was worth, as the waterlily watched it with surprise and interest.

"Well now, that little fellow got his wish after all," thought the waterlily. "Let's see if it enjoys itself more than before."

*   *   *

Two days later, the dragonfly flew over and sat on the waterlily's flower.

"Oh, you're back, are you?" asked the waterlily. "Will I be seeing you around now? I thought maybe that you were too refined to greet your old friends."

"Hello," said the dragonfly. "Since I grew up so beautifully here, I'd like to deposit my eggs. Is it okay if I leave them somewhere?"

"Oh, you'll find somewhere to put them," replied the waterlily. "Stay for a moment and tell me if you're happier now than before when you crawled up and down my stem as a little ugly larva?"

"Well, now I'm beautiful and all I came for was to deposit my eggs," the dragonfly replied impatiently. "Do I need to repeat myself?"

She buzzed around from place to place, laying one egg here, another there, and by the time she was finished she was quite tired and settled down herself on one of the waterlily's leaves.

"Well... finished, are you?" inquired the waterlily.

"Finally, yes," sighed the dragonfly "but it was better then... much better." "The sunshine is really lovely, and it's a delight to fly around the water, but I never have the time to enjoy it. I'm so terribly busy, believe me. When I was a larva, I had nothing to worry about, apart from eating, but now I have to fly around all day to put these silly eggs somewhere. I don't have a moment to myself, not even hardly any time to eat."

"Didn't I warn you not to think life would be so good?" shouted the waterlily, gloatingly. "Didn't I predict that you would regret it?"

"Who cares?" responded the dragonfly with a sigh. "I don't have time to listen to your sarcastic remarks. I need to put more eggs down."

But as it was just about to fly away, a black starling was passing by.

"What a lovely little dragonfly," it remarked, "just a delicious snack for my nestlings."

Whoosh! The starling grabbed the dragonfly's middle with its beak and flew away with it.

"Good heavens!" yelled the waterlily, shaking its leaves with dismay. "These animals! They are a bunch of weird creatures. I'm so satisfied with the quiet, peaceful life I lead. I don't hurt anybody, and no one wants to kill me. I'm so happy…"

It never finished that thought, because just then a boat with a young girl came gliding close by it.

"What a pretty little waterlily," said the girl. "I want that one."

She leaned over the railing of the boat and tore the flower away with a hard jerk. When she got home, she put it in a glass of water, and there it stood for three days among a lot of other flowers.

"I can't figure it out," thought the waterlily on the fourth morning of being in the glass of water. "I'm not any better off than that unfortunate dragonfly."

"Oh, the flowers are all wilted now," the girl said, and without a second's thought, she threw them out the window.

And there lay the once-beautiful waterlily, on the dirty ground, with its delicate white petals all shriveled and turning brown.

Please write a review!

Authors (and translators) love hearing from their readers!

To help other readers and children find these realistic descriptions of nature by Carl Ewald, please let the translator know what you thought about the stories in this book.

Please leave am honest review on Amazon or your other preferred online store.

(If you are under 14, please ask a grown-up to help you).

Thank you!

P.S. Please mention what your favorite story was.

www.amazon.com
www.classicnaturestoriesforkids.com